Foundation Competences in Business Administration

A TEXT FOR NVQ LEVEL 1

Texts for NVQ written by Sheila May and published by Stanley Thornes:

Level 1: Foundation Competences in Business Administration
Level 2: Building Competence in Business Administration
Level 3: Building Secretarial Competence

Foundation Competences in Business Administration

A TEXT FOR NVQ LEVEL 1

Sheila May

Stanley Thornes (Publishers) Ltd

First published in 1991 by:
Stanley Thornes (Publishers) Ltd
Old Station Drive
Leckhampton
CHELTENHAM GL53 0DN
England

British Library Cataloguing in Publication Data

May, Shiela
    Foundation competences in business administration.
    1. Office practices
    I. Title
    651

    ISBN 0–7487–0535–X

Typeset by Tech-Set, Gateshead, Tyne & Wear
Printed and bound in Great Britain at The Bath Press, Avon

For Max

Contents

Part II **Building Your Job Seeking Competences** 81

Foreword

National Vocational Qualifications are making an impact on people in training, both young people embarking on their careers and those who are returning to work. Level I of the Business Administration NVQ covers the broad range of basic competences required for employment in the clerical/administrative sector.

The London Chamber of Commerce and Industry Examinations Board is accredited by the National Council for Vocational Qualifications to issue NVQ awards. The Board is pleased to see publications of books that will provide support material for those in training for Business Administration, and Sheila May's book is therefore a welcome addition.

This book will be a useful source of information and will provide invaluable opportunities for the practical application of the relevant skills at Level I. It is designed to be flexible: it could be used either for group work or by individual trainees.

NVQs are meant to enhance the occupational performance of employees, so they are equally valuable to the trainee and to the employer.

The standards which form the basis of Level I Business Administration test what people can do, not just what they know. Therefore employers know that applicants with this NVQ are able to make a useful contribution to the business, right from the start, and individuals have an ideal foundation for their careers from which to progress to Level II.

Ernest Lee
LCCIEB, 1990

Introduction

Foundation Competences in Business Administration is suitable for clerical workers, full-time college students, trainees in Employment Training and Youth Training, and others who wish to work in business administration.

The book helps to promote competence in two ways; firstly through the text, which includes procedures, advice, lists, and general rules against which routines can be checked; and secondly through the *Competence Builders*, a series of tasks for personal competence building.

A common thread of knowledge and skills runs through clerical work, but the setting in which the work is carried out and the detail and content of the daily routine varies greatly. The book takes this into account by dealing with common knowledge and skills in the text, and providing for individual circumstances in the Competence Builders.

COMPETENCE BUILDERS

Many of the Competence Builders specify the type of work to be carried out but require you to make a choice or obtain necessary information. These can be discussed with your boss or tutor. Any tasks in which your competence is already proven can be ignored. In this way the book caters for a variety of readers with differing degrees of experience and responsibility.

The Competence Builders take advantage of the fact that active involvement promotes learning and you will be developing knowledge and practising skills as you carry out these tasks. Since locating, abstracting and presenting information are necessary business administration skills, you will find that readily available facts are not always given in the book but are deliberately left for you to find out.

The Competence Builders are useful for another reason: the work produced builds up into an individual file of material which you can use and add to for your own reference. The checklists in the book can be personalised, typed and added to your file, together with appropriate leaflets, instructions and other such information. Amended and kept up to date as the need arises, your file will continue to be a valuable resource for a long time to come and one which is relevant to your circumstances.

The term 'organisation' in the Competence Builders refers to your working or studying environment, whether it be a firm, a college or a training organisation. The Competence Builders can be carried out in real or simulated conditions. Real ones are best and, if you are in college, work experience might offer opportunities for carrying out some of the Competence Builders.

Where appropriate and/or more convenient, individual Competence Builders can be undertaken as group projects. In this way you will develop group skills as well as the skills specific to the task.

QUALIFICATIONS

As you will appreciate, qualifications are important, particularly when job seeking. Courses leading to traditional clerical qualifications offered by examining bodies have long been available at colleges. Many are still available and anyone studying for them will find this book, together with a review of past examination questions, a useful means of preparation. Those on TVEI courses, working towards the Certificate of Pre-Vocational Education (CPVE) or the revised BTEC First in Business and Finance will find the book particularly relevant.

National Vocational Qualifications (NVQs) are approved by the National Council for Vocational Qualifications, and are gaining in importance. They are awarded for competent performance in work activities; where possible assessment takes place in the workplace, but can take place in a realistic simulated environment. Anyone carrying out assessment must be recognised as competent to do so by the awarding body, e.g. City & Guilds of London Institute, Pitman Examinations Institute, RSA Examinations Board, The London Chamber of Commerce Examinations Board, Business & Technician Education Council.

Competence is defined as the ability to perform work activities to the standards required in employment. It embodies the ability to transfer skills and knowledge to new situations within the occupational area. It encompasses organisation and planning of work, innovation, and coping with non-routine activities. It includes those qualities of personal effectiveness required to deal with a variety of working relationships.

NVQs are awarded at a number of levels. Credits for parts of NVQs, called units, can be accumulated in order to build up to a qualification over a period of time and at a pace to suit individual needs and circumstances. Units at different levels can be worked for simultaneously, thus allowing greater expertise in specialist areas to be accredited. There are no barriers to anyone wishing to gain an NVQ, such as age, and where or how competence was acquired.

There is no requirement for NVQ candidates to have followed any particular type of course or training programme before undertaking assessment for the qualifications. Anyone can therefore reach competence through on-the-job training, experience, college courses, distance learning, private study, or a combination of these.

A number of foundation competences have been agreed by the Administrative, Business and Commercial Training Group, after wide consultation with industry, commerce and the public service, trade unions, the education service and other organisations, as representing the critical achievements for trainees in reaching occupational competence. These competences form the basis of National Vocational Qualifications in Business Administration at Level 1. At this level competence is recognised in the performance of a range of work activities which are primarily routine and predictable or provide a broad foundation for progression.

Statements of competence, called elements, have been grouped into units, and these equate with Units 1–9 in this book (see the appendix for a list of elements against which are shown the page numbers for the relevant Competence Builders). Following this text and working through the Competence Builders will therefore help you to develop competences for the NVQ Level 1 qualification in Business Administration. Many of the elements are integrated in the Competence Builders since real work-based situations, in which practice and assessment are best carried out, do not consist of neatly separated sets of tasks. Each Competence Builder clearly indicates which of the main elements the tasks will help you to become competent in (see the appendix for details of what the reference numbers refer to). In addition to the NVQ requirements, Units 10, 11 and 12 in this book give help to those who are not yet working or who are considering a change of job.

The performance criteria, against which your competence will be assessed, can be found in 'Standards of Performance for Administrative, Business and Commercial Staff', available from The Training Agency in Sheffield. If you are at college or in training, your tutor should have a copy. You will find it useful to refer, in this publication also, to the underpinning skills and knowledge needed for competence and the range of variables to which each element applies. This will help you in self-assessment. In judging your own competence you should realise that assessment will be made on the basis of the successful day-to-day *consistent* demonstration of competence. Consistency is of prime importance in determining that occupational competence has been achieved.

Using the book and working through the Competence Builders will help those already in work, those attending a college or training course, and others who wish to make a career in Business Administration, to lay a firm foundation which can be built upon for progression to levels 2, 3 and beyond.

Part I

Building Your Office Competences

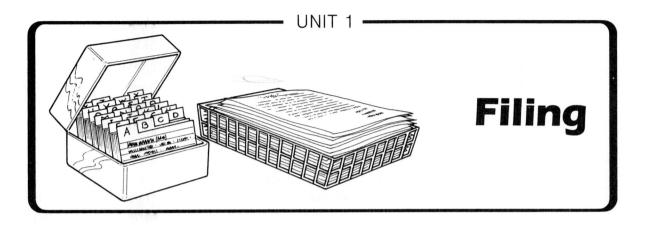

Filing

A considerable amount of information is received in offices. Some items can be consigned to the wastebin but much has to be kept for future reference. Filing systems are therefore set up not only to ensure that records are kept safely, neatly, and in a manner that protects their confidentiality, but also so that they can be found swiftly and easily.

The term 'filing' is generally used to cover the sorting and putting away of documents, the retrieving of them, and the recording of file and document movements. 'Doing the filing' is one of the most important tasks that a clerical worker has to do. Incorrectly filed records are as good as lost, and this can lead to delay, frustration, an increase in costs, loss of goodwill and even loss of business.

Unfortunately, since much of the actual work associated with filing is routine, its importance tends to be forgotten and the work is not always carried out as well as it should be. Every person, no matter how junior or senior, who has access to a filing system, must be knowledgeable about it and aware of the importance of using it correctly.

FILING DOCUMENTS AND OPENING NEW FILES

In order to be able to 'file to find' you must follow a classifying system which determines the order in which files are stored. There are several such systems, with the alphabetical and numerical being the most commonly used.

Competence Builder 1
(Elements 1.1, 1.2)

Find out about the filing systems in your organisation. Which ones are you likely to have access to or be required to work on? What is the system of classification used?

Alphabetical Filing

This is a popular method. A file is made out for each name and these files are then arranged in strict alphabetical order. For each letter of the alphabet there is also a 'miscellaneous' file into which papers of insufficient quantity to warrant individual files are placed. These miscellaneous files are often used for separating the batches of files for each letter of the alphabet, but there are other means – such as lettered cards (guide cards) – for doing this.

The major advantage of the alphabetical filing system is that it is simple to manage without any need to refer to an index. A disadvantage is that it is difficult to assess how much space needs to be allowed for the addition of new files. This can result in space being wasted or time being spent in shifting files and reorganising cabinets.

A more serious disadvantage arises from people not keeping to a standard system of strict alphabetical order. It is necessary therefore to adhere strictly to a set of rules so that everyone using the system knows where to find a file. The following rules generally apply, although companies have their own variations:

▶ If an organisation's name is a person's surname, then the first letter of this decides the order, followed by subsequent letters in that name and, if necessary, by the accompanying initials preceding the name, e.g:
Anderson, B
Anderson, G
Andrews, A
Bacon, K
Baker, D

▶ If the organisation's name consists of several surnames, the first decides the filing position, e.g:
Ayers, Allington & Aldridge is filed under Ayers.

▶ Even if an organisation's name is not a surname, alphabetical order is still used, but unimportant items like 'The' are ignored, e.g:
The Abbey Building Co. is filed under A – Abbey Building Co., The.

▶ Initials standing alone are usually filed first, e.g:
BFSC Ltd comes before Babylon Freight Services Co. Ltd.

▶ Names beginning Mac, Mc, or M are all filed as though they were Mac, e.g:
M'Intyre
McMorris
MacWinter

▶ Prefixes such as O', De, De La and Van are treated as part of the surname which follows, e.g:
Delaney
De La Rue
De Trafford

▶ Names beginning with S' or St are filed as if they were spelt Saint, e.g:
S' Leon
St Mathilde
Saint Patrick

▶ There is a filing rule 'Nothing comes before something', which is used as a reminder that where surnames are the same those without an initial precede those with one initial, which in turn precede those with two initials, e.g:
Jones
Jones, J
Jones, J J

▶ In hyphenated names the first name is used, e.g:
Willoughby-Jones is filed under W.

▶ For impersonal names, such as government departments, the name under which the organisation should be filed is that which distinguishes it from others, e.g:
The Department of the Environment is filed under E – Environment, Department of the.

▶ Titles should be ignored when items are placed in alphabetical order, but they are written after the surname and before the Christian name, e.g:
Sir Roland Jeeves is filed under J – Jeeves, Sir Roland.

Competence Builder 2 *(Elements 1.1, 1.2)*

a) Learn the rules concerning alphabetical order.

b) Make a list of the names of all the people you know, and the names of all the famous people you can think of. Go through a newspaper adding further names to increase the number to about 75. Add the names given in the alphabetical rules. Place each one of these names on a card or piece of paper. Put them into alphabetical order. Check your order by referring to the rules.

c) If you are a student, or in training, ask your tutor for some past Office Practice examination papers. These often contain lists of names to be put into order and are useful for practice.

d) When you have practised sufficiently to be confident, ask to prove your competence by pre-sorting the filing on a number of occasions for a section of your organisation where the files are kept in alphabetical order.

Numerical Filing

This system is particularly useful where new files are being opened regularly. New files are placed at the back of the existing ones, so expansion is no problem.

Consecutive numbers are allotted to correspondents. An alphabetical index is kept, showing the number of each file. When a file is required, it is necessary to refer to the index in order to obtain its number.

Apart from ease of expansion, there are other advantages: numbered files are easier to find than alphabetical ones, and are less likely to be misplaced when refiled; the file number provides a useful reference and, if this is used on letters, there is no need to refer to the index.

There are also disadvantages. Although a numbered file can be found more easily than an alphabetical one, you must first obtain the number from an alphabetical index. This takes time, as does keeping the index up to date. You must also take care not to transpose numbers (e.g. 87 instead of 78). This can lead to serious misplacing of records.

Competence Builder 3   *[Elements 1.1, 1.2]*

Place a different number (chosen randomly from numbers 1 to 200) in the top right-hand corner of each of your alphabetical cards/papers (see Competence Builder 2b). Now re-sort these cards/papers into numerical order.

Chronological Order

Papers within each file are normally placed in chronological (or date) order. It is usual to place the most recently dated item on the top and the oldest on the bottom. Chronological order is also used for bring forward (follow up) systems. These cater for instances where jobs have to be done or requests met at a certain time, but where the papers concerning them are not likely to be needed before-hand. They are therefore filed away and a reminder system is set up to ensure that the papers are 'brought forward' at the time required.

Cross-references

If documents could logically be filed in more than one place, then some form of cross-referencing needs to be used. This is to ensure that the documents can always be found, regardless of which of the alternative places the searcher looks in. A convenient way of cross-referencing is first to decide under which of the names the papers will be filed, if necessary seeking help from someone who might require the papers at some future time. Make out this file and then another for the alternative name. Leave the alternative file empty, but place a note on or inside it referring anyone looking for the papers to the file which contains them.

Competence Builder 4   *(Elements 1.1, 1.2)*

If you are studying or training with a group and several of you have carried out Competence Builders 2b and 3, put three persons' sets of cards/papers together and take it in turns to sort them firstly into alphabetical order and secondly into numerical order. Check each other's work on this, referring to your tutor in cases of doubt. Which of the two classifying systems did you find it easier to sort under?

General Rules for Filing Documents

A filing system is only effective if everyone who is authorised to use it does so efficiently. The following general rules promote efficient filing practices and help to make filing less time-consuming:

▶ File daily – particularly if other people are also using the files. A wrong decision could be made because the most up-to-date papers were sitting in the 'To be filed' tray. Filing at the same time each day helps to instil this as a habit and ensures that the job is done as a matter of course.

▶ Follow your organisation's system for checking that all papers have been cleared for filing. An example of such a system is that papers ready for filing are initialled. If any papers are not so marked, guidance must be sought from a more senior person.

▶ Circle, underline in red, or otherwise highlight the name under which papers are to be filed. This helps to avoid error and speeds up the filing. However, marking up can become automatic and you should take care that mistakes do not occur as a result of your not giving enough attention to the job.

▶ Staple related papers together. Do not file paper clips as they add bulk and other papers get caught in them. Remove pins because they cause injury.

▶ Sort papers into batches in the order in which they will be filed. Remember that if a person is writing from an organisation then the correspondence is filed under the name of the organisation, not under the writer's name.

▶ Speed your sorting. If the classification system is an alphabetical one and a sorter is available – use it. If a large quantity of numerically classified papers have to be filed, these can be roughly sorted by first putting all the thousands together, then sorting each pile of thousands into hundreds, then tens, then the exact order.

▶ Check that every paper is placed in the correct file. Misfiled papers can cause untold trouble and loss to an organisation.

▶ Check that every paper is placed in the correct order in the file – chronological order with the most recent document on top.

▶ Place papers neatly and squarely in the folders. It is easier to do this by taking the file folder out, rather than by attempting to slide papers into it.

▶ Where needed, make out new files and label them neatly and clearly. If you are working on a numerical system make sure you place the new file name on the alphabetical index.

▶ Check miscellaneous files every time you file anything in them. If there are several items for one correspondent (say five or six), and it appears likely that contact will continue, make out a separate file.

▶ Make cross-references wherever there is a possibility that papers might be looked for in more than one place.

▶ Renew folders when they become worn – or at least make a note to do so when you have time.

Competence Builder 5　　　　　　　　　　*(Elements 1.1, 3.1)*

Type up your own version of these rules for reference. Extract the key point only from each rule and include only those appropriate to your circumstances.

IDENTIFYING AND RETRIEVING DOCUMENTS

If you are asked to produce a file for another member of staff, remember that work might be held up until the file is found. You should therefore locate the item and pass it to the person concerned promptly. Should there by any delay, then that person must be notified and the reason for the delay be given. Problems can of course arise if you receive several requests at the same time. People need to be kept informed as to how long they might have to wait. You will probably find that you have to be careful in dealing with those who cannot wait their turn, and it might be that you have to agree with your boss some system for meeting file requests. If you are given deadlines, you must organise and plan your work to meet them.

When papers are required from the filing system, remove the whole file concerned – otherwise another person may use the file not realising that it is incomplete. A booking out system should be used.

Booking Out Systems

There are a number of systems used to ensure that files can be traced when they are absent from the filing cabinet. Without such a system much irritation, waste of time and costly delay can occur.

One system uses 'absent folders'. These should be of a different colour from the normal file folders to make them stand out. One of these is inserted in place of a file being removed. Into it is placed a form showing the name or number of the removed file and who has it. Adding the date encourages people to return files as soon as possible. The absent folder can be used for placing papers in whilst the actual file is out. Although convenient for this purpose, it can cause problems because the person using the file is without the most up-to-date papers and these might affect the work that person is doing, or decisions which have to be made. A safer practice to follow is to take additional papers as they come in to the person who has the file.

A similar system uses a card for each absent file on which is recorded who has the file. The card is placed where the file would normally be.

Another alternative is to record file movements in a register. The advantage of this is that it can readily be seen which files are out and for how long. Chasing up files and requesting their prompt return then becomes easy.

Competence Builder 6   (Elements 1.2, 2.3, 3.1, 7.1)

What is the system in operation in your organisation for the borrowing of files? Type out instructions, or make a photocopy of any printed ones.

METHODS OF FILING FOLDERS

Lateral and vertical methods are the most common for the filing of folders, but each has advantages and disadvantages.

Lateral Filing

The file folders are placed side by side on open shelves, or in cupboards, or are suspended in pockets from rails. The pockets are fitted with title holders which are sometimes angled to make it easier to read the file names. Difficulty in reading these is one of the disadvantages of this method.

Another disadvantage arises from one of the advantages – that of being able to build filing shelves up to the ceiling. This saves space, but retrieving files from a height is a safety hazard which needs to be guarded against by using firm step-ladders and taking care.

The major advantage of lateral filing, space saving, is further achieved because space does not have to be left to allow for the opening of drawers, as is the case with vertical filing.

Vertical Filing

The file folders are arranged, usually in cabinet drawers, so that they are standing upright. Their titles can be seen clearly, and papers can be looked at without removing the folders.

Standing the file folders in a drawer does mean that they are subject to a lot of wear and tear. To prevent this 'pockets' are often used. These are fitted together concertina fashion, suspended from metal runners fitted inside the drawers. Placing folders inside these pockets not only protects the files and keeps them neat, but also provides a place for an absent card or folder when a file is borrowed.

There are safety hazards associated with this type of filing also. These usually arise from carelessness. See Unit 9, Health and Safety, to find out how to guard against these hazards.

Competence Builder 7   *(Elements 1.1, 1.2, 2.3)*

a) Pre-sort and file documents in a real or simulated established system, opening new files as directed and cross-referencing material as needed. Seek guidance where necessary in order to ensure that the documents are classified and filed correctly.

b) Identify and retrieve documents, passing them to the correct person or location.

c) Carry out booking out/in procedures.

d) Trace missing or overdue files.

METHODS OF FILING OTHER RECORDS

Some records which have to be filed will not fit into a conventional file folder. These include large plans and drawings, for which drawers and specially fitted cabinets are available, and cards.

Card Filing

Cards are commonly used to provide an index for a filing system where direct access is difficult, for example, a numerical system (which usually needs an alphabetical index). They are also used for record keeping systems in their own right. Stock records, accounts records, customer records and mailing lists are a few examples of the types of information for which cards are convenient.

Cards which are not referred to frequently can be kept filed vertically in a box or small drawer. Cards which are in frequent use are more convenient when placed in flat or rotating trays or fixed to the centre of a wheel which is rotated to bring the required card in view. A visible card index system has a number of useful features – see Unit 5 for an explanation of its use as a stock record system.

Competence Builder 8   *(Elements 1.1, 2.3)*

Set up your own filing system to use for filing the information you gather and produce as a result of working through the Competence Builders in this book. You will find this personal set of files useful for reference and it is one which you can continue to add to for a long time to come. If you produce paperwork as a result of proving some of your competences by means of simulation, or keep records over a period of time to show the external verifier, you will find your filing system useful for this too.

SAFETY AND SECURITY

▶ Never walk away from a filing cabinet leaving a drawer open. This could be walked into or tripped over.

▶ Never open more than one drawer at any one time. This can cause the filing cabinet to overbalance.

▶ Never use a chair or some other makeshift item in order to reach high shelves where files are stored. Always use steps, or similar, especially provided for the purpose.

▶ Maintain the security and confidentiality of files and documents. Filing cabinets containing confidential information should be kept locked at all times. Other filing cabinets should be locked at night.

Competence Builder 9

(Elements 1.1, 1.2, 3.1, 9.1)

a) On a card type out the safety rules given here. Add the rules relevant to filing from Unit 9. Keep this card on your desk, referring to it constantly until you know you carry out the rules automatically.

b) Find out who is permitted access to the various filing systems in your organisation. Type this out in the form of a list, adding a note of the means of ensuring confidentiality which file users are required to follow.

c) Find out if there is restricted access to any of the files which you have to handle and ensure that they are always kept secure.

d) Find out what the policy of your organisation is in regard to the long-term retention of files and documents.

Much of the efficiency of an organisation depends on the ability of its staff to access records without delay. This is only possible if all involved have dealt with the filing correctly. You should never underestimate the importance of being careful when dealing with 'the filing'.

Communicating Information

People communicate in business in order to pass on and exchange information. Much of this communication is less effective than it could be. Too much fails completely; much of it causes irritation. Often it fails to promote a good impression of the organisations represented by those communicating.

COMMUNICATING BY TELEPHONE

The telephone is a powerful, immediate means not only of conveying information but also of creating impressions. You will almost certainly use it frequently and must remember when doing so that you are 'the organisation' to the person on the other end of the telephone line. If you are curt or rude, then an unfavourable impression of your organisation will be formed. If you are courteous and considerate, then the impression is likely to be favourable.

In face-to-face encounters there are a number of 'props' available to help promote a favourable image: the provision of magazines, attractive floral arrangements and decor, comfortable chairs, the pleasant manner and welcoming smile which you can personally add. When speaking on the telephone these props are not visible but the pleasant manner and the smile are still very important. A 'smile in the voice' is not just word play – it really does come across.

Telephone Manner and Using Your Voice Effectively

The way in which you use your voice is all important on the telephone since it is the sole means of communication. Adopt a cheerful, warm, friendly tone and be considerate and sympathetic in your manner. A word of caution though – be friendly, but not over-familiar. Business relationships and communications are fast becoming less formal, but the degree of informality acceptable varies from one person to another, and from one organisation to another. The safest approach to adopt is one which is businesslike without being curt, and which conveys a willingness to help combined with knowledge of the job. This assures people that they are being dealt with efficiently.

Clarity is important when speaking on the telephone, with consonants emphasised and the sound neither too loud nor too soft. Speaking in a dull monotone is boring to listen to and best avoided. You can do this by modulating your voice – that is changing the pitch. If you start a sentence in a low pitch your voice will rise naturally and you can bring it down again for the next sentence or comment. The female voice, being naturally higher pitched than the male one, should be pitched deliberately lower for telephone use.

Aim for a calm, relaxed, unhurried tone, with good enunciation. You should be competent in the 'spelling out' of place-names or difficult words using the telephone alphabet (see Figure 2.2, p.32).

Words with the same vowel sound, such as five and nine, can sound alike and you need to be especially careful when quoting figures, names and unfamiliar words. If the listener cannot hear, it is preferable to speak more distinctly rather than more loudly. It helps to cup the hand round the mouthpiece. Always speak straight into the mouthpiece – not across it, as this distorts the sound and allows background noise to be heard.

Never eat or drink whilst using the telephone. Avoid slang such as 'OK', 'right-oh', 'half-a-tick' and 'tarrah'. Do not address people as 'love', 'me duck', or similar.

Competence Builder 1
(Elements 2.1, 3.1, 7.1)

a) Either photocopy or type a copy of the telephone alphabet shown at the end of this Unit (Figure 2.2) for your own use.

b) Role play a number of telephone calls during which it becomes necessary to use the telephone alphabet, until you are competent.

PROCESSING INCOMING BUSINESS TELEPHONE CALLS

It is essential for everyone using a telephone system to be familiar with the equipment, and with the organisation's approved procedures. Only then can calls be handled effectively.

When receiving a direct outside call, the name of the organisation is given first – 'Jones and Dean' – so that the caller knows immediately that he or she has obtained the right number. 'Good morning' or 'Good afternoon' can follow.

A call should always be answered promptly. Once answered it must be dealt with equally promptly. Apart from unnecessary expense, a delay might be an inconvenience for the caller – especially for someone in a callbox with a limited amount of change, or a phonecard with not many units left on it.

Callers should always identify themselves immediately. Some don't, and start a conversation straight away. If this happens, you should not interrupt the caller, but should try to obtain a name as soon as there is a pause. You can then establish the caller's requirements and deal with the call yourself or transfer it to some more appropriate person.

Transferring Calls

It is important to recognise when you cannot adequately deal with a call. It is equally important to know who can do so, and where that person works. For a caller, being transferred and retransferred when trying to obtain some information or deal with a query is irritating and this must not be allowed to happen. Neither must contact be lost, leaving the caller in limbo getting more and more agitated.

Being transferred quickly and competently usually impresses a caller and enhances the reputation of the organisation. You should therefore aim to be able to use the equipment effectively and know the location and responsibilities of people in the organisation.

Competence Builder 2   *(Element 2.1)*

Use the equipment available in a real or, where necessary to provide the variety of telephone calls, in a simulated environment to carry out the following operations:

a) identify callers and establish their needs,

b) transfer calls to alternative internal extensions,

c) deal with callers who have got the wrong number,

d) deal with misdirected calls,

e) diagnose and report any equipment faults which might occur,

f) carry out the routine cleaning of equipment.

Tact and Diplomacy

Tact and diplomacy are needed in handling the varied situations that arise on the telephone. This is especially so if the person asked for declines to accept a call. In informing the caller, aim to give the impression that the call would be taken if it were at all possible. If you need to be firm, be so politely. The caller may not be welcome at that time, but circumstances change and today's unwelcome caller may be tomorrow's welcome one!

Tact is also needed on occasions when it is necessary to 'cover up' for someone, albeit for a legitimate reason. Callers should not be told, 'X is not back from lunch yet', especially in the middle of the afternoon, or 'Y hasn't arrived yet.' The one suggests that lunch is taking a longer time than it ought and the other that the person is late again! It is sufficient to say, 'X is not in the office at the moment' and offer to put the caller through to someone else or to take a message.

Sometimes callers refuse to give a name, possibly because they know that their call is unlikely to be accepted. A polite but firm refusal to pass on a call, stating that the person asked for will not speak to anyone who does not give a name, is reasonable.

There may be occasions when people ask to speak to a certain person about matters which someone else deals with, and you have to suggest putting them through to the alternative person. Diplomacy is needed in order to prevent people feeling that they are getting second best.

Meetings are not normally interrupted by telephone calls, nor is a person disturbed when an important visitor is present. That person's secretary will usually take a message and hand it over afterwards.

The greatest advantage of the telephone – instantaneous communication – is at the same time its greatest disadvantage. It is liable to be an unwelcome disturbance. However, a caller cannot know when it is the worst possible moment for someone to be taking a call and should not be made aware of it. You have to be very careful not to convey irritation. Since the voice is the only point of contact, the listener tends to have a heightened awareness of the other person's feelings as well as of the words used.

The telephone is not an accurate medium for conveying intended impressions. Sounding hurried, for example, does not necessarily give the impression of being busy – it is more likely to give the impression of being disorganised and not able to deal adequately with the matter being discussed.

Everyone recognises that brevity is essential if telephone costs are to be kept down. It is therefore perfectly acceptable to be brief without in any way indicating that you would prefer not to be bothered with the caller at that particular moment – no matter how true that might be.

Even when the telephone interrupts you frequently, you have to remember that each time it is a different caller. Any information given or requested must receive as much care and attention as if it were from the only caller of the day. Ideally, the person at the other end of the line should feel just that.

Dealing with Aggressive Callers

People often behave more aggressively on the telephone than face to face. Sometimes this is because it is easy to misjudge a response when the other person's reactions cannot be seen. Sometimes it is because people feel braver knowing that a call can be terminated if it becomes too difficult.

In dealing with irate people you should never reciprocate their bad temper. It doesn't help, it causes further aggravation. Staying calm usually has the effect of cooling the situation and you can gain satisfaction from having kept your self-control.

It has to be accepted that telephone calls do not always run smoothly. You must be prepared for people who are rude, impatient or unpleasant in some other way. In some cases they might be justified! You must simply be determined to be pleasant and polite, always bearing in mind that the words used and the tone you adopt affect the response received from the other person.

Giving Information

You will sometimes be asked to provide information on the telephone. Not only does this require you to be knowledgeable about all aspects of your work, it also requires you to know from where, or from whom, information can be obtained. It further requires you to be able to determine correctly what it is that people want to know. A problem here is that people are often not really clear about this themselves! Listening carefully, asking questions in order to clarify anything about which you are not sure, is essential if you are to avoid wasted time and frustration both for your caller and yourself.

In using the telephone, and indeed in all your conversations both in and outside the organisation, you must always be aware of what you can disclose and to whom. Always be on your guard against being pumped for information and do not gossip carelessly about your work. Much important commercial knowledge is passed to competitors in this way, and the efficiency of any organisation's security measures for safeguarding information depends to a large extent on its staff.

Competence Builder 3   *(Elements 2.1, 2.3)*

Under simulated conditions:

a) answer on the telephone questions relevant to your work or studies (some of the questions should require you to have to look up information),
b) deal with callers who are pressing very hard for information which must not be divulged,
c) deal with the situation where the person asked for has declined to speak to the caller,
d) deal with a caller who refuses to give his or her name,
e) deal with a caller who is behaving aggressively.

Note: Two or more of the above situations might arise naturally as part of the same telephone call.

When a Caller is Holding On

Time on the telephone is expensive. If a call has to be left for an enquiry to be made, or some information found, then the caller should be informed how long this is likely to take, and be asked to call back in a stated length of time. This avoids unnecessary costs being incurred and also prevents snippets of conversations being overheard. If asking the caller to ring back is not practical, then there must be an adequate means of 'muffling' the telephone – some systems play music whilst callers are on 'hold'. Calling back or being called back is, however, the best alternative. It saves money, and the inconvenience to others of lines being engaged.

In these days of rising telephone costs, company policy sometimes dictates whether or not you offer to phone callers back or ask them to call back. It can depend on the caller's status.

Competence Builder 4

(Element 2.1)

a) Cost the following telephone calls:

▶ 5 minute **local** calls at peak, standard and cheap rates,

▶ 5 minute **a** band calls at peak, standard and cheap rates,

▶ 5 minute **b** band calls at peak, standard and cheap rates.

b) To what periods of time are peak, standard and cheap rates applied?

PROCESSING OUTGOING BUSINESS TELEPHONE CALLS

Careful planning is essential for the efficient use of the telephone. This involves keeping an index of regularly used telephone numbers, together with relevant dialling codes. *Yellow Pages* and other classified directories are best kept near to the telephone of anyone who has frequent need of them. Keeping calls short, making them at the cheapest time, jotting down points to be discussed and collecting papers likely to be needed beforehand all help to keep costs down.

Competence Builder 5 *(Elements 2.1, 2.3, 3.1)*

a) Familiarise yourself with the information pages of the local telephone directory, in particular check up on how to obtain local, national and international calls.

b) Familiarise yourself with *Yellow Pages* and other classified directories available. Find out and keep a note of the name and number of the taxi service nearest to your organisation. During what hours does this service operate?

c) Type up instructions for reference on how to contact: the Operator, Emergency Services, Directory Enquiries, and how to use the Freefone and Telemessage services.

d) Look up in a telephone directory the number of a firm whose name you have been given by your boss or tutor and obtain the dialling code.

e) If you do not have one already, compile a frequently used telephone numbers' index for business or personal use. Look up and include codes.

When making a call, state at the outset what it is about. This puts the person receiving the call mentally in the picture. If there are a number of items to be discussed it is helpful to say how many there are. This methodical approach will convey itself to the other person and, if the information that follows is put across concisely and precisely, will create an image of efficiency.

If you obtain a wrong number, you need give only a brief apology before hanging up. It is rude not to apologise, but equally annoying to the other person to be given a long explanation.

If disconnected during a conversation it is up to the call initiator to ring again. Following this rule ensures that both parties are not ringing each other simultaneously, thus finding the lines engaged.

You should send a letter confirming a call as soon as possible afterwards if the matters discussed were important, or if there is a possibility that written confirmation might be required for reference or evidence.

Competence Builder 6   *(Elements 2.1, 2.2, 2.3, 2.4)*

a) Obtain appropriate details from your boss or tutor to enable you to compose an accurate and legible letter confirming a telephone call.

b) Determine the purpose of operator services such as Alarm Calls and Fixed Time Calls. Obtain for your personal reference file the information leaflet regarding these and other operator services (see telephone directory).

c) Under real or simulated conditions:
   - ▶ make an ADC call,
   - ▶ establish calls on behalf of other people and transfer the calls,
   - ▶ make a number of calls concerning your own work or training.

Telephone Answering Machines

These are in common use for taking messages when there is no one to answer the telephone. When you leave a message on an answering machine, speak clearly and at normal speed. You should expect to give your name and that of your organisation, and your telephone number. It is also helpful to state the time of your message, especially if it is an urgent one.

Competence Builder 7   *(Element 2.2)*

Leave a message on an answering machine. This should include instructions for someone to follow which will enable you to know whether or not your instructions were clear.

RECEIVING AND RELAYING ORAL AND WRITTEN MESSAGES

Communicating via a third person is common in the business world and you will frequently find yourself in the position of either sending a message or relaying one on behalf of someone else. Messages are sent within and outside an organisation. To be competent in the taking and recording of oral and written messages, from internal and external people, both in person and by telephone, you need to use a number of skills. These include being able to:

▶ communicate effectively both orally and in writing,

▶ establish rapport and goodwill with colleagues and clients,

▶ listen effectively,

▶ use questions effectively to check understanding and seek additional information.

You will need to know who people are in your organisation, what their responsibilities are, and where they can be found. Procedures vary for passing information and it is important that you find out, and adhere to, those which are acceptable in your organisation.

Oral Messages

Oral messages are frequently relayed and/or received incorrectly and the fault can lie with any or all of the people involved.

People sending messages are often not clear in their own minds about what they want to convey, or what they want to achieve as a result of the message they are sending. Even when they are sure about this, they often do not express themselves clearly. They also tend to concentrate on themselves rather than on making sure that the person who is to relay their message has understood it. The person for whom the message is intended might not listen attentively, or might not understand the message but not wish to show ignorance of some matter by questioning it.

What can you, when in the position of being the relayer of a message, do to ensure that it is received as intended?

▶ Listen carefully – both to the message and to any instructions regarding it.

▶ Write the message down, or at least the key points.

▶ Ask questions about anything that is not clear.

▶ Repeat the message back to the sender.

▶ Make sure that you know who the sender is.

▶ Check that you know for whom the message is intended, and where that person can be found.

▶ Determine how urgent the message is.

▶ In passing on the message make sure you relay it exactly, without any interpretation of your own.

▶ If face to face with the message receiver, look for signs of understanding.

▶ If the message is complicated ask if you should repeat any part of it. This could apply particularly on the telephone.

▶ If the person to whom you have to give the message is not available leave a written message in preference to passing it on by means of another person.

▶ If you have to leave a written message make sure that it is accurate, unambiguous, legible, grammatical, and that the tone, style and vocabulary are appropriate.

Competence Builder 8   *(Elements 2.2, 8.1)*

a) Discuss with your colleague(s) or fellow student(s) a message which you delivered for someone recently. What was it intended to achieve? Was this clear to you? Can you be sure that it was clear to the person to whom it was communicated? Could the message or the means of communication have been improved? Bear this Competence Builder in mind when you are asked to convey messages and make sure that they reach their destination as intended.

b) At work, during work experience, or whilst on placement, ask for opportunities to take oral messages to be passed on in writing, and to accept written messages to be passed on orally, for example on the telephone. These opportunities might arise as part of your normal duties.

Written Messages

The need to relay a message in writing might arise as a result of your being asked to pass on a message within your own organisation, from someone visiting in person, or from your taking a telephone message.

Taking messages on the telephone is a frequent necessity, so it is time-saving to cultivate an automatic response. Since messages entrusted to memory can be forgotten, or important details be omitted, you should write them down immediately. For this purpose many organisations use pre-printed forms (see Figure 2.1). These should be kept where they are immediately available – either on the desk or on the top of a drawer – together with a pen or pencil. Shuffling around for paper or pencil conveys an impression of inefficiency and increases the cost of telephone calls unnecessarily. Ideally, telephone message forms should be located on the right-hand side for a right-handed person, with the telephone on the left, and the opposite for a left-handed person. It is a good idea to read messages back before the end of a call to confirm accuracy. Place messages prominently on the desks of the people for whom they are intended to ensure that they are seen immediately they return.

Competence Builder 9   *(Elements 2.1, 2.2, 3.1, 7.1)*

If you are not already doing so as part of your daily routine, take a variety of telephone messages under simulated conditions. Pass the messages on using your organisation's pre-printed forms. If these are not available design your own, type up a master copy, and reproduce a quantity on whatever reprographic facilities you have available.

```
┌─────────────────────────────────────────────────────────────┐
│                        MESSAGE                               │
│                                                              │
│  For Gordon Day               Date 10/5/19– Time 10.15       │
│                                                              │
│   ┌─────────────────────────────────────────────────────┐   │
│   │  NAME Mr S Houghton                                  │   │
│   │  COMPANY Well's Toy Co Ltd                           │   │
│   │  ADDRESS 67 Fairway St. Downtown                     │   │
│   │  TEL. No. (0592) 64318  TELEPHONED ☑ CALLED ☐        │   │
│   └─────────────────────────────────────────────────────┘   │
│                                                              │
│  MESSAGE:                                                    │
│  He now has available the samples you wished to see and      │
│  could call to see you any time next week.                   │
│                                                              │
│                                                              │
│   ┌─────────────────────────────────────────────────────┐   │
│  ACTION:  │ WILL RING AGAIN ☐    WILL CALL AGAIN ☐       │   │
│  (S)HE    │ IS WRITING ☐                                 │   │
│           ├─────────────────────────────────────────────┤   │
│           │ PLEASE RING NUMBER ABOVE              ☑      │   │
│           └─────────────────────────────────────────────┘   │
│                                                              │
│  TAKEN BY Susan James                                        │
└─────────────────────────────────────────────────────────────┘
```

Figure 2.1 Message form suitable for telephone messages and those left by personal callers

Listening

Listening is a very important skill in receiving messages. This might seem obvious, but many people are not good at it and seem to make no effort to improve. This is probably because they consider listening to be something we are able to do from birth. Not actually true! What we are born to do is *hear*, which is not the same thing. Listening requires active participation and attention, and problems arise because our attention wanders and distractions get in the way.

Much of the working day is spent listening and much irritation results when it is done badly. It is therefore worthwhile trying to develop competence in this. Here are a few suggestions:

▶ Work hard to try to keep up with what is being said and do not react to distractions.

▶ Concentrate on what is being said rather than on what you are going to say in reply.

▶ Do not jump in too quickly with a response – there might be more to come which will help your understanding.

▶ Ignore grammatical errors that people make, but check that you have the content right.

▶ Ask questions to check your understanding.

Competence Builder 10 *(Elements 2.1, 2.2, 8.1, 8.2)*

Quite often people who are good communicators in other ways are deficient as listeners. Critically assess your own performance as a listener. Discuss this with your boss or tutor, a colleague or a friend. Apply any suggestions offered where appropriate.

SUPPLYING INFORMATION FOR A SPECIFIC PURPOSE

You will often be asked to supply information and will find that much of your reputation as a competent clerical worker will depend on your ability to do so, including meeting any deadlines set.

In most cases you will not be expected to be carrying the details in your head but you must know where to obtain them from. Being able to tap into reference sources, informal as well as formal, is therefore an essential competence for you to achieve.

The first place to search for information should always be amongst the records of your organisation which are in everyday use, or to which there is easy access. These will include records stored in files, on cards and lists, on microfilm and in computer files. These immediate sources of reference should automatically yield information on matters in general use such as those to do with customers and suppliers.

Colleagues can usually be called on for information. In addition to being easily available, they may also be familiar with the matter about which you are seeking information and/or have records which can be referred to.

Competence Builder 11 *(Elements 2.3, 8.2)*

List six departments or staff in your organisation. State by the side of each the main areas of information you could expect to obtain from them.

You might have to contact people outside the organisation in order to obtain the information required. You will thus need to find out what communication services are available in your organisation. Take all the opportunities presented to develop your skills in using the equipment, e.g. telex, fax. This will help you later when working towards the Level 2 competence 'Transmit and receive copies of documents electronically'.

Televised Information

This provides another information source which might be available within your organisation. Information is brought up on the screen of a television receiver, or similar equipment, upon accessing a computer databank service. This might be a private service operating within a closed circuit, or a public one such as those operated by the television companies and British Telecom. Stock market reports, foreign exchange rates, news headlines, air services and other travel information, including weather maps, are examples of the type of information available by this means.

Competence Builder 12 *(Element 2.3)*

a) Have you got the television companies' teletext services available via your home television receiver? If so, look at them; if not, arrange to see them elsewhere. Make a note of the major categories of information available.

b) Find out what information is available via British Telecom's Prestel service.

c) Are you authorised to obtain information from any source in your organisation with which you are not yet familiar? If so, ask for instruction and opportunities for practice.

Libraries

Some outside sources of reference are readily accessible. The library service is an obvious one, and using all its facilities effectively is yet another essential competence for you to build up.

Libraries are often thought of primarily as places from which books can be borrowed, and many people are not aware of the wealth of information that can be found in reference sections. Reference books cannot be borrowed but notes can be made from them and there is often a machine available for copying small amounts of material, which is permitted without infringing copyright.

Competence Builder 13   *(Elements 2.3, 7.1)*

Visit your local library and find out the regulations which apply to the photocopying of information from books. Keep a note of these in your personal file for reference when required.

You need to be familiar with the Dewey Decimal indexing system. This is commonly used in libraries and familiarity with it allows rapid access to the books you want without the need to consult library staff. It might still be necessary, however, to seek help in the reference section unless you are familiar with this. Library staff are also usually willing to give information over the telephone, and it might not be necessary for you to make a visit in order to obtain a small specific item of information.

Competence Builder 14   *(Element 2.3)*

Familiarise yourself with the Dewey Decimal system of indexing. In which section and amongst which numbers would you expect to find this book? Is it in your local library?

Reference Books

Some of these are dealt with elsewhere in this book in the relevant sections. Other books which you will find useful will depend on your organisation's work and the responsibilities of your job. You should expect those which need to be referred to regularly to be available at your workplace.

Competence Builder 15 *(Elements 2.3, 3.3)*

a) Make an alphabetical list of the reference books, directories, catalogues, etc., that you might be required to refer to in your organisation. Negotiate an opportunity to look at all of these and familiarise yourself with the contents. Add to each reference source on your list a note of where it is normally kept and a brief summary of the contents.

b) Ask your boss or tutor for work which will give you practice in locating information from a variety of sources including, where available, computer files and microfilm.

Other Sources of Information

Information is often best obtained from a specialist in that field, for example:

▶ banking matters from a bank,

▶ employment matters from the Department of Employment local office,

▶ motor vehicle matters (driving licences and tax) from the Driver and Vehicle Licensing Centre at Swansea, and vehicle tax in certain circumstances from post offices,

▶ National Insurance matters from the Department of Social Security local office.

Competence Builder 16 *(Element 2.3)*

Write or type out this list of other sources of information. Discuss it with your boss or tutor or with colleagues and ask for their suggestions in order to provide yourself for future reference with a comprehensive list of sources appropriate for your work.

Passing on Information

Information must be passed on as promptly as possible to those who have requested it, making sure that any stated deadlines are met. Any difficulty in doing so should be reported immediately this is realised. The means chosen for passing on the information should be the most appropriate – letter, telephone, telex, fax and face-to-face conversation – unless this has been specified.

General points to observe in passing on information are:

▶ All sources must be acknowledged.

▶ Copyright or other legal requirements must be observed.

▶ Security, and procedures to ensure confidentiality, must be followed where appropriate.

DRAFTING ROUTINE BUSINESS COMMUNICATIONS

Your written material should be perfect in presentation and content, not only because this creates a good impression, but also because it is often kept as a permanent record. For perfect presentation you must follow the guidelines and formats laid down by your organisation. For perfect content you must make sure not only that what is stated is accurate but also that the spelling, punctuation, use of English, and the manner in which people are addressed, are all correct.

Spelling

Dictionaries are generally underused and undervalued and yet people continue to misspell. Sometimes this is because they do not recognise an incorrect spelling and therefore see no reason to check it. There can also be problems in using a dictionary if a person's idea of the spelling is too far out, for example 'foney' instead of 'phoney'.

Even when people recognise that they have a spelling problem they often accept it as something over which they have no control, saying, 'My spelling is dreadful!' Certainly it can be a problem, but it is one which must be turned into a competence for anyone working in business administration. If it is a problem for you, then reading, practising the spelling of words you know you have difficulty with, obtaining a copy of the most commonly misspelled words and practising a few of these each day will help. Do not rely on electronic typewriters and word processors which have built-in spelling checks. They are not always available and are not a satisfactory substitute for personal spelling competence, which can be used anytime, anywhere.

If you are uncertain of the meaning of a word when reading, it does not necessarily mean that you cannot understand it without using a dictionary. This is because the context in which a word appears usually gives sufficient indication of its meaning. It is, however, still worth looking the word up as a check and as a way of bringing it into your usable vocabulary.

Competence Builder 17   *(Elements 2.2, 2.4)*

a) If you have not got them already, obtain dictionaries for use at work and at home. Look up every word you come across where you are not sure of the spelling or meaning. Do this conscientiously and you will soon find that you can use correctly words that once you were uncertain about.

b) Ask anyone for whom you produce written material not only to correct any errors but also to point them out to you. This is a good way to help you to learn. Practise and use frequently any words with which you have difficulty until you can use them perfectly.

Punctuation

The use of punctuation is often a problem in writing but you need it in order to break up the flow of words, to add emphasis and to help understanding. Think of punctuation as something which compensates for the fact that in writing you cannot otherwise pause and convey meaning in the ways that you can when speaking.

There are certain rules of punctuation which you have to learn and follow, although taste and common sense are also involved. Since clarity and ease of reading is the purpose of punctuation, the better it is used the less obtrusive it will be. Although there are a number of important punctuation marks, just the correct use of the basic full stop and comma will bring about a dramatic improvement in your writing if these have previously caused difficulties.

Competence Builder 18   *(Elements 2.2, 2.4)*

Set yourself the objective of learning and mastering the basic rules of punctuation. Learn a rule and consciously apply it in all your writing. When its use becomes automatic, move on to another rule. In this way you will build up to full competence.

A book to help with the use of English, with awkward points of grammar, for instance, is useful to have at hand. Fowler's *Modern English Usage* is an example.

Planning

There is no secret for success in writing and it is not easy. Learning appropriate rules, then hard work and practice are what are needed in order to build competence. One rule which stands out above others is that writing must be planned, and this begins with the obtaining of all necessary information followed by the arranging of this into an ordered and logical sequence.

Appropriate Language

Written words often seem more authoritative than spoken words, and of course much written material is filed away as a permanent record. Perhaps it is an awareness of this which prompts people to write in a formal manner, particularly in business. This is neither necessary nor desirable. Business correspondence is best written with the points made as briefly as possible, using common rather than uncommon words and avoiding the pomposity of what is known as 'Business English'. Old-fashioned phrases like 'Assuring you of our best attention at all times' still linger on, but really have no place in modern business communications. Similarly, common long-winded ways of saying things are often unnecessary. A well-known example is 'at this moment in time'. Why not use 'now'? Remember that brief, simple and to-the-point writing encourages people to read it.

Some forms of communication such as the memorandum and letter are set out in a standard manner. If your organisation has laid down guidelines regarding format, style, vocabulary, and rules as to who should sign the documents, you should follow these. If there are no such guidelines, you should use commonly recognised conventions.

Memoranda

A memorandum or 'memo' is used within an organisation to request or pass on information. This means of internal communication is chosen rather than the spoken word for specific reasons: for convenience, if it is intended for several people, or because a written record is needed.

Pre-printed forms are commonly used. A salutation is not required – that is a person is not addressed 'Dear . . .' – as in a letter, neither is there a complimentary close such as 'Yours . . .'. A signature is not required either, but this, or initials, is helpful since it indicates that the memo has been checked by the sender.

Memos often concern several people. If this is so it is usually addressed to the person it most concerns, or the senior person. 'C' or 'copy' is typed at the bottom of the memo, followed by a list of those who are to receive it. The memo is then circulated, with people ticking or crossing out their names before passing it on. An alternative, and generally better, method of distribution is for copies to be taken and distributed to everyone at the same time.

Although memos should be as brief as possible they should, for the sake of clarity, be written in complete sentences – not in note form. A good general rule is: one subject, one memo. This simplifies its filing under a subject heading. If you ever have difficulty in deciding where to file a memo when this rule has not been followed, then take a photocopy to file under each of the possible subjects. Each set of records will then be complete.

Competence Builder 19 *(Elements 2.4, 3.1)*

Type your own version of the information given regarding memoranda. Find out and incorporate anything specific to their use in your own organisation.

Letters

Inevitably an organisation is judged by the letters it sends out. This means that the tone must be appropriate, the spelling and punctuation without error and the presentation perfect.

The tone of a letter should be appropriately formal for people not known, more informal for those known. If a letter is in reply to another, then the tone of the original is a useful guide.

Rules for Letter Writing

▶ Always use letterheaded paper.

▶ Include in every letter the name and address of the recipient, the date, the correct salutation and complimentary close.

▶ Address the letter to a person by name when known.

▶ When answering a letter which gives a reference, refer to this in the reply or type it before the name and address of the recipient, e.g. 'Your ref GLF/Sales'.

▶ When answering a letter, acknowledge its receipt – 'Thank you for your letter of 6 January . . .' – briefly refer to its subject matter and answer any questions asked.

▶ Consider referring to the subject matter of a letter by giving it a title. This usually appears after 'Dear . . .'.

▶ When writing to confirm details previously discussed, state what these are.

▶ Plan a logical sequence – 1. Introduction, and reason for letter being written; 2. The subject matter; 3. The action looked for.

▶ Start a new paragraph for each new topic.

▶ Ensure that each point follows naturally from the previous one and leads on to the next.

▶ Avoid jargon, abbreviations, or anything else which might not be clear to the reader.

▶ In writing, adopt a businesslike style with short paragraphs and short sentences. Use punctuation correctly but sparingly.

▶ Use the correct close. If the letter is addressed to a person by name, close with 'Yours sincerely'. If the letter is not addressed to a named person and begins, for example, with 'Dear Sir', close with 'Yours faithfully'.

▶ Refer to any enclosures in the body of the letter and add 'Enc' at the bottom.

▶ Avoid adding postscripts. These are for afterthoughts and letters should be planned in advance!

▶ Always follow laid down security and confidentiality procedures in dealing with correspondence.

▶ Update any records on which a note of correspondence has to be kept.

Competence Builder 20   *(Elements 2.3, 2.4, 7.1)*

a) If you are not doing so already, ask for the opportunity to compose and draft a variety of routine memos and business letters incorporating both text and numerical information. This could include letters of enquiry, acknowledgements to communications, confirmation of business arrangements and appointments for interview, and a variety of memos and letters providing information. The essential information for these should have to be located and obtained from a variety of sources.

b) Discuss this work with your boss or tutor and make photocopies of good examples of your work to keep in your file.

A for Andrew	J for Jack	S for Sugar
B for Benjamin	K for King	T for Tommy
C for Charlie	L for Lucy	U for Uncle
D for David	M for Mary	V for Victor
E for Edward	N for Nellie	W for William
F for Frederick	O for Oliver	X for X-Ray
G for George	P for Peter	Y for Yellow
H for Harry	Q for Queen	Z for Zebra
I for Isaac	R for Robert	

Figure 2.2 Telephone alphabet. When it is necessary to emphasise a letter or spell out a word, it can be done by using an alphabetical code as shown above.

UNIT 3

Data Processing

Data is the term used to indicate raw facts which can be in the form of words, letters, characters and numbers. Data processing is the term commonly used to describe work on the computer in converting data into useful information. This can include storing, locating and sorting data, doing calculations and making simple decisions. Data processing is, however, a loosely applied term and in this unit it includes not only work on a computer but work on any alpha/numeric QWERTY keyboard.

PRODUCING ALPHA/NUMERIC INFORMATION IN TYPEWRITTEN FORM

The QWERTY keyboard is an integral part of many office machines. Dedicated word processors, computers, telex, phototypesetting and desktop publishing machines, as well as typewriters, all have this arrangement of keys. The increase in QWERTY keyboard equipment has naturally led to an increase in the number of people using it, and means that keyboarding skills are desirable for many workers who would not think of themselves as typists.

This section deals solely with the level of skill required by such people, for example those who use a keyboard for producing a screen display, with a printed copy as required, and those who type documents and letters to a limited extent. It can, however, also be looked on as a means of acquiring elementary skills by those who wish to progress later to the level of competence required of secretaries, typists and word processor operators.

The knowledge and skills needed to underpin competence in using a keyboard to produce typewritten information are:

▶ the layout of the QWERTY keyboard,
▶ the operation, and safe and correct use of the equipment (including the diagnosis of faults),
▶ recognised fingering techniques,
▶ the best posture in order to reduce fatigue,

▶ how to care for the equipment and any routine maintenance procedures that you have to carry out,
▶ how to use the facilities available for printing,
▶ the use of the most efficient and effective methods of error correction on the equipment available,
▶ how to check spellings and references in dictionaries and appropriate reference sources,
▶ how to plan the layout of the work,
▶ how to use the facilities for saving information.

Safety and Care

You must ensure that you operate all equipment in a safe manner and that you do all you can to safeguard yourself and those with whom you work. You should never touch any equipment until you have been trained in its use. You should also recognise that when you are keyboarding you need to take precautions in order to minimise fatigue, and also precautions to minimise eyestrain when using a visual display unit (see Unit 9).

In order to minimise fatigue you should pay attention to good posture, ensuring that your back is well supported by the chair and your trunk is relaxed with a slight forward lean. Your feet should be firmly on the floor and your elbows slightly out from the sides. The level of your hands and the curve of your fingers will vary according to the design of the keyboard, but your wrists should be kept down. Your fingers must do the work with the minimum of movement of your wrists and arms.

Competence Builder 1
(Elements 3.1, 9.1)

a) Familiarise yourself with the equipment you have to operate. Even though you should have been shown how to use it, still read through the user's manual identifying each part and reminding yourself of its function. Find out from your boss or tutor what maintenance procedures you should carry out, and what and to whom you report in the event of fault or breakdown.

b) Refer to Unit 9, Health and Safety, and type a note of the points given which concern keyboarding equipment.

Technique

Even if you consider keyboarding as just a useful additional skill, one which will not occupy much of your working day, it is still important to be as competent and efficient as possible. It is therefore worth persevering in learning to touch type, that is to type keeping your eyes on the copy and not on the keyboard. In doing this you keep your fingers over what are called the 'home' or 'guide' keys. These are keys a, s, d, f for the left hand, and j, k, l, ; for the right hand. Keys g and h are left free in the middle. It helps your concentration in learning to touch type if you say each letter to yourself as you type it. Try to maintain an even rhythm in striking the keys.

Skills must be practised as often as possible. Aim therefore for frequent short practice sessions rather than occasional long ones. If you find you have a particular problem, such as jumping capitals (caused by incorrect timing of the shift key), then concentrate on practising this.

Competence Builder 2 *(Element 3.1)*

a) Familiarise yourself with the QWERTY keyboard. Obtain or borrow a copy of a typewriting manual and practise the fingering shown until you can use automatically the recommended fingering for each key.

b) If you have word processing equipment, find out what facilities are available for printing. If there is a choice, determine the quality of printing available and under what circumstances you should use each of the choices.

If you persevere, you will find that you will be able to type keeping your eyes on the copy. Not only does this save time, it also avoids the risk of the common inaccuracies which arise from taking your eyes off the copy – the repetition and omission of words. It also reduces mental and physical fatigue.

Typing Letters, Envelopes and Memos

The typing of letters, envelopes and memos follow laid down conventions in regard to layout and spacing. You will find these laid out in typewriting manuals together with ample material for practising your skills. You will find that there is more than one acceptable layout, but you should always follow your organisation's guidelines as a first choice.

Error Correction

Checking your work on a continuous basis, say after each paragraph, allows you to make corrections more easily. Recheck at the end of each page. Even if you do not check until you reach the end of the page, you should always do so before taking your work out. This is because it is often difficult to align a correction after returning the page to the machine. The practice you need in correcting errors depends on the equipment. Some will require little skill on your part, others quite a lot, but the overall result must be that the error correction is unobtrusive.

Competence Builder 3

(Element 3.1, 3.2)

Find out what correction facilities are available on the equipment you have to operate and practise using these until your corrections are acceptable to your boss or tutor.

You will need to practise your keyboarding skills until you can consistently produce approximately 150 words or numeric equivalents in a ten-minute working period with a maximum of two uncorrected spacing or typographical errors, and all errors corrected must be unobtrusive. This will meet the performance criteria for competence at this level, but you must of course strive to ensure that you reduce your number of errors and that none are left uncorrected. Also, both in order to prove your competence, and in your regular work, you must ensure that:

▶ faults are identified and dealt with in accordance with the manufacturer's instructions and/or promptly reported,

▶ security and confidentiality of information is always maintained.

Competence Builder 4

(Element 3.1)

Negotiate with your boss or tutor for opportunities to practise at a QWERTY keyboard until your production of letters and memos (combining text and numeric data) and envelopes fulfils the performance criteria. When you can do this consistently you can ask for your competence to be assessed.

IDENTIFYING AND MARKING ERRORS ON SCRIPTED MATERIAL FOR CORRECTION

In addition to checking your work as you go along, you also need to proof read it thoroughly on completion. Do not be misled into thinking that there will not be any errors left to find – we are surprisingly blind when it comes to noticing our own mistakes. This is a competence which has to be worked on and developed to the extent that errors are so apparent it is as though they were highlighted.

If you are studying in a group, check each other's work for practice in proof reading material you have not produced yourself. There is a task you are likely to be asked to carry out on occasions and is a competence you therefore need to develop.

When found, errors should be marked clearly for later correction, either by yourself or some other person, using recognisable correction signs. In doing this, whether it be your own or someone else's work, you should look out in particular for:

▶ common spelling errors, for example, 'stationery' (writing materials) when 'stationary' (meaning 'still') is intended,
▶ keyboarding errors,
▶ the omission of words, numbers or punctuation,
▶ words or numbers transposed, e.g. 67 instead of 76.

You should also check:

▶ that the layout conforms to the specification,
▶ that, in the absence of specific instructions, the format and style accords with that generally used by the organisation,
▶ any spellings about which you are uncertain,
▶ the spelling of names,
▶ the accuracy of calculations, clearly identifying any errors or omissions.

Finally, you should report anything about which you are uncertain, and make any necessary amendments as directed.

In checking your own work, or that of other people, you should make use of a dictionary or calculator as needed. Moving a ruler down a page under each line helps to ensure that errors do not pass unnoticed. Using a sheet of paper achieves the same purpose with the added advantage that it screens your eyes from the distraction of what comes later on the page.

Anything complicated should be checked by two people. If one of them has produced the work, he or she reads the original and the person who has not been previously involved checks the work. This is to guard against the common danger already mentioned – that of not noticing your own errors.

When proof reading on a visual display unit (VDU), you might find that it helps to place your finger against the screen and move it along as you check each word. You need especially to check that you have carried out all the required functions when word processing. It is very easy to miss small additions or deletions and special instructions. A very high standard of proof reading is essential before printout, because some errors, such as spacing faults, are easily missed on a VDU.

Competence Builder 5
(Element 3.2)

a) Always check your own work carefully before passing it on.

b) If you are not already familiar with the correction signs employed in your organisation, obtain a copy of them.

c) Arrange with your boss or tutor for opportunities to practise your checking skills on business documents such as handwritten and typewritten drafts and printouts. Ask particularly for numerical material because great care is needed in checking this.

UPDATING RECORDS IN A COMPUTERISED DATABASE

Computers are used in many everyday situations in the office, for example, for stock control, wages, and several of the tasks concerned with buying and selling. A major advantage of computers for these tasks is that a large amount of data can be stored and processed in a very short time.

Competence Builder 6

(Elements 3.1, 3.3)

a) Find out for what purposes computers are used in your organisation.

b) Find out the procedures laid down by your organisation for maintaining the security and confidentiality of information. Type a note of this for your file.

Basic Facts and Terms

You will find it helps to know a few basic facts, and recognise what is meant by some of the terms used. Two terms in general use in connection with computers are 'hardware' and 'software'. Hardware refers to the components and units which make up a computer. Software refers to the programs, data and information which a computer uses. To get information in and out of a computer there are operations called 'input' and 'output'. Input is the operation of entering data into a computer, for example, by using a keyboard. Output is the operation of getting information that has been processed out of a computer, for example, by printing it. Computers have to be told what to do with the data and these operating instructions are called 'programs'. The processing of the data takes place in the part of the computer known as the central processing unit (CPU).

You might find a mini-computer or a mainframe at work, but the computer with which you are most likely to be already familiar, the microcomputer, is used in many offices. This is because microcomputers are compact, low on power consumption, and cheap. They consist of a keyboard for inputting the data; a television-like screen on which the accuracy of the data input can be checked and on which the output information is displayed; and a printer for producing a paper or 'hard' copy. Computer 'printout' is another term. Flexible plastic disks, sealed inside protective covers, are a common means of storing data and programs not in use.

Computer File Handling

A file is an organised collection of related records. An example would be a firm's employee records organised in alphabetical order. These records might include (in addition to people's names) their home addresses, telephone numbers (if any), dates of birth, works' numbers, rates of pay, and the names of the departments in which they work. These details may change, more records may need to be added, others deleted. The modifying of a file is called 'updating', and it is in this that you need to become competent. You must also be able to use the data in the file by reading one or more records, for example in order to find out someone's address. This is called 'accessing the file'.

The records on the file in the example contain a number of separate items of data, i.e. address, telephone number, etc. These subdivisions of a record are known as 'fields'. All records in a file must have the same number of fields and the data on each record must be in the same order. This means that if the first field of the first record holds the name of the employee, then it is in the first field of all other employee records that employees' names will appear. The second field of every record will similarly hold the same information about each employee, e.g. home address and so on. The same number of fields must exist for each record, even if some do not contain any data. This would happen on records in the example where an employee did not have a home telephone (see Figure 3.1).

	Record 1	Record 2	Record 3	Record N
Field 1 (Name)	Dyson Brian	Jones Roy	King Chris	Young Tony
Field 2 (Address)	2 John St	70 Green St	14 Field Cres	9 Dean Rd
Field 3 (Tel no)	—	76149	52582	72471
Field 4 (Subscription – Sports Club)	—	75	—	—
Field 5 (Subscription – Union)	150	150	—	150
Field 6 (Holiday Fund)	300	—	500	—

Figure 3.1 Computer file

Competence Builder 7 *(Elements 2.3, 3.3)*

If it is not already part of your work, negotiate with your boss or tutor opportunities for you to learn and practise the following computer activities:

▶ accessing a program,

▶ entering text/data using all necessary keys and commands,

▶ checking inputted text on screen to detect and correct errors,

▶ searching/sorting and retrieving specified information,

▶ saving text/data,

▶ copying text/data file to another disk/backup data file disk.

The activities listed in Competence Builder 7 are those which you will be required to carry out when your competence is assessed. In your practice sessions you should aim to meet the performance criteria against which you will later be judged. This means:

▶ always accessing the correct field,
▶ correctly transcribing and entering data into appropriate fields,
▶ always maintaining security and confidentiality of information,
▶ promptly reporting faults or failures and accurately describing symptoms,
▶ following operating and safety procedures at all times.

Competence Builder 8   *(Elements 3.1, 3.3, 8.2, 9.1)*

a) Ask for help and/or information if you are not completely familiar with the safe operation and care of the equipment you are using, and if you are not totally knowledgeable about any common faults and their symptoms.

b) Type up and keep in your personal reference file a note of your organisation's preferred styles and formats, including file-naming conventions.

c) Discuss with your boss or tutor your competence in planning and organising your work, and in meeting deadlines. If necessary make a concentrated effort to improve. If you have a serious problem, determine with your boss or tutor why this is and what can be done about it. If you have no problems – well done!

Processing Petty Cash and Invoices

In business, the payments for goods and services must be entered in some form of financial record keeping system, and the documents used must be commonly accepted. Petty cash is a simple example of such a system, and the invoice is one of the most common documents. They are likely to be used by everyone in business administration and you need therefore to be knowledgeable about the systems and competent in processing the documents.

PROCESSING PETTY CASH TRANSACTIONS

Money must always be accounted for, and someone must be accountable for it. This applies to small amounts as well as to large. Not only must money be accounted for but it must be seen to be so – in other words there must be a recognised system.

Small items of expenditure for which cash is used are usually accounted for by means of a petty cash system. These items include: telephone calls outside the office, bus fares, cleaning materials, postage stamps, magazines, flowers, etc. In each case the individual amounts are small but the total amount of cash being handled can add up to a considerable sum. Only by operating a system is it possible for every penny to be accounted for. Since cash is of value to everyone, ways of protecting it against theft must be determined and be strictly observed.

Security Rules

▶ Irregularities should be reported immediately to an appropriate authority.

▶ Cash must never be left lying around, no matter how little there is of it, or for how short a period of time.

▶ Cash must be kept in a locked box which in turn is locked away in a cupboard or drawer. When the box is in use it must not be where others could touch it.

▶ The keys to the box, and the cupboard or drawer where it is kept, should be held by the person responsible for the petty cash. There does of course have to be provision for absence of that person so that petty cash requests can still be dealt with. Whatever the arrangements, access to the keys must be limited.

▶ Any change to be given should be counted out and handed over before the money tendered is put away. This avoids the possibility of a mistake being made, for example giving change for a different value note. It also makes it impossible for anyone to claim falsely that they have been given the wrong change.

▶ Money should be counted out in front of, and paid directly to, the person claiming it in order to avoid any later claims of error.

▶ Accurate and up-to-date records of all monies, in and out, must be kept.

▶ The forms used and the cash movements against them should be doubly checked to make sure that they match.

▶ There should never be any mixing of petty cash and personal money for the purpose of providing sufficient 'change' or as a temporary borrowing – either way. This can lead to error and charges of dishonesty, however innocent the intention.

Competence Builder 1   *(Elements 3.1, 4.1, 7.1)*

a) Find out the categories of expenditure for which petty cash is used in your organisation.

b) Find out the security rules that apply in your organisation regarding safety of the petty cash. Type up a copy or photocopy any existing document regarding this to keep in your file.

PETTY CASH SYSTEM

The petty cashier is given a sum of money, known as the imprest or float, which is estimated to be sufficient to cover petty cash requirements for a given period of time – a week or a month. During this period money is handed out on receipt of petty cash vouchers. This means that the cash in hand, plus the value of the vouchers, always adds up to the total of the imprest.

A petty cash account is maintained throughout and this is balanced at the end of the period. The petty cashier then draws a sum of money equal to the stated expenditure in order to restore the original imprest. The system continues in this way, with adjustments made to the imprest if it is found to be unrealistic.

Petty Cash Vouchers

Petty cash vouchers are usually pre-printed and numbered. On these is written the date, what the cash is required for, and the amount. A voucher is required whenever a payment has to be made or an item purchased from petty cash money. The voucher is completed, signed by the person requiring the money, and countersigned by a senior member of staff empowered to authorise the expenditure (see Figure 4.1).

Petty Cash Voucher	Folio _CB2/89_
	Date _20 Feb_ 19–

For what required	AMOUNT	
Stationery	5	66
VAT		85
	6	51

Signature _S. Higgins_

Passed by _G. M. Needham_

Figure 4.1 Petty cash voucher

Sometimes an item is purchased before the money is drawn from petty cash. In this case the person making the purchase must obtain a receipt and hand this in, along with a petty cash voucher, as a claim for refund of the money spent. Receipts should be obtained, wherever possible, for all petty cash items. They are attached to the relevant petty cash vouchers, which are filed after being entered in the petty cash account.

Competence Builder 2 *(Element 4.1)*

Discuss with your boss or tutor:

a) what, as a petty cashier, would cause you to ask questions or refuse to make payments when requested

b) how you would file petty cash vouchers. Justify your suggestion.

Petty Cash Account

A petty cash account has columns for the date, details of cash received, details of cash paid out, and what are known as analysis columns which are headed in accordance with each main class of expenditure – postage, stationery, office expenses, travel, etc. The petty cash voucher number appears alongside the item to which it applies. The amounts paid out appear twice – once in the amount paid column and again in the appropriate analysis column. Using analysis columns makes it easier to total each class of expenditure separately at the end of the petty cash period (see Figure 4.2).

As well as totalling the columns, the petty cashier must also balance the account and check that:

▶ The analysis columns' totals added together equal the total of the amount paid column. If they do not, then there are errors, probably due to carelessness, and these must be corrected.

▶ The cash in hand shown in the petty cash account equals the cash in the cash box. If it does not, and no error can be found in the account, then this should be reported.

Competence Builder 3   *(Elements 4.1, 7.1)*

a) In a real or simulated situation, carry out petty cash procedures including:

▶ maintaining security procedures,
▶ checking vouchers, including correct authorisation,
▶ completing petty cash account with voucher details,
▶ storing vouchers and receipts,
▶ balancing petty cash and petty cash account,
▶ totalling expenditure,
▶ presenting petty cash account and cash in hand for checking,
▶ topping up imprest to agreed level when needed.

Note: i) Practise and/or demonstrate your ability to use a calculator where appropriate.

ii) If it is necessary to set up a simulation, and you are studying or training with a group, then work this Competence Builder together. Take turns as petty cashier, with the others producing vouchers and making requests for cash. Base the items of expenditure on the information gathered in Competence Builder 1a). Make enquiries of the cost of these goods and services in order to determine realistic amounts for which to make out the petty cash vouchers.

b) If petty cash vouchers and petty cash account forms are not readily available, obtain or make a master and reproduce a supply of these forms to a standard acceptable for use within your organisation.

PETTY CASH ACCOUNT

Dr.   **Cr.**

CASH RECEIVED			CASH PAID				ANALYSIS				
Date	Folio	Amount	Date	Details	Voucher No.	Amount Paid	Stationery	Postage	Travel	Office Expenses	VAT
Feb 1	CB2	7 21		Balance b/d							
		42 79	–	Cash received							
			Feb 2	Cleaning windows	82	11 50				10 00	1 50
			„ 5	Flower vase	83	2 99				2 60	39
			„ 7	Envelopes	84	4 29	3 73				56
			„ 9	Postage	85	6 60		6 60			
			„ 13	Fares	86	1 22			1 22		
			„ 14	Coffee	87	1 87				1 87	
			„ 16	Milk	88	3 00				3 00	
			„ 20	Stationery – miscellaneous	89	6 51	5 66				85
			„ 21	Biscuits	90	48				48	
			„ 23	Postage	91	2 45		2 45			
			„ 28	Fares	92	76			76		
						41 67	9 39	9 05	1 98	17 95	3 30
			„ 28	Balance c/d		8 33					
		50 00				50 00					
Mar 1	CB3	8 33		Balance b/d							
		41 67		Cash received							

Figure 4.2 Petty cash account

Value Added Tax

Value added tax (VAT) is not paid on everything, including a number of items for which petty cash is commonly used. The total VAT for this account can thus be quite small. VAT is shown in a separate analysis column on a petty cash account and this usually appears on the extreme right-hand side. The amount of VAT paid is stated in this column and then deducted from the total cost of the item. The sum left is placed in an analysis column according to the expenditure category.

PROCESSING INCOMING INVOICES FOR PAYMENT

Invoices are accounts sent by suppliers indicating the monies due for goods or services supplied. When regular orders are placed, the supplier uses the invoice to advise the buyer of the cost of supplies rather than as a request for immediate payment. A typical invoice consists of a letterheading with the name, address, telephone number, and similar details, of the supplier. It is dated, and the buyer's name, address and order number are typed on it, followed by details of the transaction. The items are totalled to give the amount payable.

When an invoice arrives from a supplier its details are checked against the order and the delivery note, and the calculations are checked. Any errors or discrepancies are reported and should be dealt with immediately. Invoices which are correct can then be passed on for payment. Credit and debit notes are similarly checked.

Processing documents at all stages is facilitated by numbering and cross-referencing, for example order numbers are stated on invoices, and invoice, credit and debit note numbers appear on statements.

Competence Builder 4   *(Elements 1.1, 2.4, 4.2)*

a) In a real or simulated situation, check invoices for accuracy, and against order and delivery notes, reporting any discrepancies and errors promptly.

b) Ask your boss or tutor for an opportunity to:

▶ draft a letter of complaint when next there is a discrepancy in an invoice sent to your organisation,

▶ draft a letter of apology, assuming the receipt of a letter of complaint from a customer who has received an incorrect invoice from your organisation.

If necessary b) can be a simulated exercise.

Suggest where copies of these letters might be appropriately filed. In doing this work for real, bear in mind the importance of confidentiality.

BUSINESS DOCUMENTS

The transactions of buying and selling are made formal by a sequence of documents which, although individual in appearance, are standard in content and use. It will help you in processing invoices to know how they relate to these other documents. Figure 4.3 shows these documents and their movement between buyer and supplier.

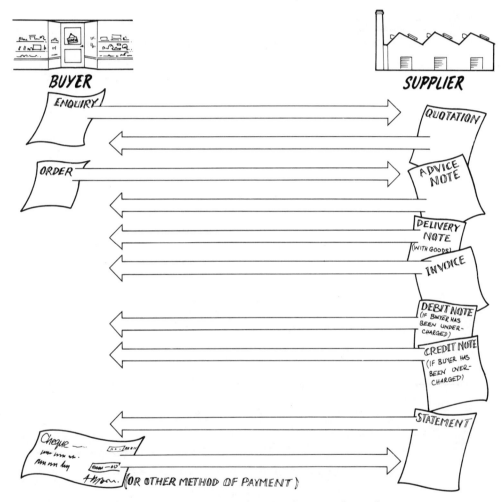

Figure 4.3 Movement of business documents between buyer and supplier

Competence Builder 5 *(Elements 3.1, 4.2)*

Draw up your own version of the chart above. Carry out this task using a typewriter or computer with a word processing programme and use it as an opportunity to practise/demonstrate your keyboarding skills.

Enquiry

This is the initial contact between a prospective buyer and a supplier. It can be by means of a letter or a form from the buyer asking the supplier for a price for supplying the goods and services required, and for related information such as a delivery date. A prospective buyer usually contacts more than one supplier in order to have a choice when placing an order.

Quotation

This is sent from the supplier to the prospective buyer in response to the enquiry. It sets out the information requested – often on a pre-printed form – and will state exactly what can be supplied, the delivery date, price and terms of payment. It is also usual, where the enquiry is for a regularly stocked item, for catalogues and price lists to be sent in response to an enquiry.

Order

Once a supplier has been selected, the buyer sends an order to that firm. On the pre-printed order form will be boxes or sections for a description of the goods or service, and any catalogue or reference number, the quantity required, the price, terms of payment and delivery arrangements. As is usual with all forms used in the process of buying and selling, the form will be numbered and dated, and both the buyer's and the supplier's name and address will appear. The order form has to be signed by a person authorised to do so. Sometimes the supplier will send an acknowledgement of the order. This is most likely to happen when the goods cannot be despatched, or the services performed, immediately.

Competence Builder 6   *(Elements 2.2, 4.2)*

Under real or simulated conditions, complete an order form on appropriate stationery with full essential details from information taken during a telephone conversation.

Advice Note and Delivery Note

If the goods are to be despatched by rail or post, then an advice note is usually sent by the supplier to advise the buyer that the goods are on their way. A delivery note accompanies the goods. If the goods are being delivered by the supplier's own transport, then the driver will have two copies of the delivery note. One copy is left with the goods, the other is signed as a receipt for the goods and returned to the driver. If the goods are not inspected on delivery, then it is important that the copy of the delivery note returned to the driver has a note added – 'Goods received unchecked.' The goods are later checked against the delivery note to ensure that what has been delivered is as stated. A check that there is no damage will also be made at this stage if it has not been done previously.

Debit Note and Credit Note

If a buyer has been undercharged for goods – either in error or because of a price change – a debit note is sent by the supplier. If a buyer has been overcharged a credit note is sent. A credit note is also used if goods are returned to the supplier either because they are not wanted or because they arrived damaged. If packing cases have been charged for on an invoice, then a credit note will be issued on their return to the supplier.

Statement

A statement is issued by the supplier at regular intervals, usually monthly, as a request for payment. It lists all the invoices, debit and credit notes issued since the previous statement, and shows any payments received. The balance is the amount the buyer must pay.

Competence Builder 7   *(Elements 2.1, 3.1, 4.2, 8.2)*

Organisations have separate departments for dealing with buying (purchasing department) and selling (sales department) if the volume of work warrants this. There will also be an accounts department or someone responsible for this work.

a) Add to the knowledge you have gained of the functions of a purchasing department by reading or, preferably, talking to someone working in one. Type up notes stating these functions and add descriptions, in your own words, of the main documents used by this department.

b) Carry out the same tasks as in a) for a sales department.

c) Carry out the same tasks as in a) for an accounts department.

Stock Handling

In every organisation someone has to be responsible for the storage and control of stationery and other office consumables such as cleaning materials and refills for beverage dispensers. Stationery stores for the modern office carry more than the paper items and small pieces of equipment traditionally associated with the term. In them can be found tapes and disks for typewriters, word processors and computers, chemicals, toner, and similar materials for machines such as copiers.

Although much of the work involved is routine, it is nevertheless vital to the effective running of an office that it is carried out competently. Record keeping must be without error to ensure that items are available on request; security must be tight since petty pilfering is common; housekeeping must be efficient because paper goods in particular are easily damaged and costs are high; and there must be a constant regard for health and safety, including adhering to regulations regarding the storage of hazardous materials.

Competence Builder 1

(Elements 5.1, 9.1)

a) Refer to Unit 9, Health and Safety. Make a note of every aspect relevant to the receipt, handling and storage of stock.

b) Find out what hazardous materials are kept in the stationery store in your organisation.

ISSUING OFFICE MATERIALS ON REQUEST

The number of people required for dealing with office consumables, and how frequently supplies are issued, will largely depend on the size of the office staff.

Where numbers are large, then looking after the store can be a full-time job, with the store open for handing out items throughout the working day. Where there are few office workers, then someone might deal with the stock for only a few hours each week, with a deputy to cover absences and a more senior member of staff to carry overall responsibility.

For an efficient system, with a minimum of waste, there must be strict rules, including the days and times when supplies are issued. This might be once or twice a week or every day. A greater frequency is more convenient for office staff and reduces the number of occasions on which someone 'cannot possibly wait' until the correct time for the issue of stores. Against this has to be set the too-frequent interruption of other duties which the person dealing with stores has to carry out, and some reasonable compromise needs to be agreed.

The frequency of issue of supplies will determine the amount held by each person or department. This should always be sufficient to last until the next issue, plus some in hand. Only in an exceptional emergency should it be necessary to ask for items to be issued other than at laid down times.

Competence Builder 2 *(Elements 5.1, 9.1)*

Make notes on:

a) the duties of office stock keeping in your organisation,

b) the procedures for handling potentially hazardous materials (see Competence Builder 1b).

Be prepared to prove your knowledge by answering questions on this from your boss or tutor.

Requisitions

Another strict rule is that supplies are only issued against a written requisition. This is usually a pre-printed form on which is written the description, reference number and quantity of the item wanted, and by whom. It is dated and should be signed by a responsible person such as the head of a department (see Figure 5.1).

The requisition can be taken along to the store at the appointed opening time and the items waited for. A more efficient system is to have the requisitions placed in a box, or posted through the door of the store, by a laid down time. The store's clerk then collects up the items in accordance with the requisitions and distributes them to the staff concerned. There are other variations possible on these routines. What is important is that there should be an established routine and that this is adhered to.

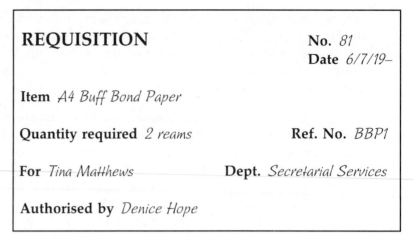

REQUISITION   No. *81*
                                   Date *6/7/19–*

Item *A4 Buff Bond Paper*

Quantity required *2 reams*   Ref. No. *BBP1*

For *Tina Matthews*   Dept. *Secretarial Services*

Authorised by *Denice Hope*

Figure 5.1 Stationery requisition form

MONITORING AND RESTORING STOCK LEVELS

To ensure that stocks are always available it is essential that they do not fall below a minimum level. This level is the amount needed to last for the period between ordering repeat supplies and their delivery. Equally important to work to are maximum stock levels. This is because stock ties up money. Maximum stock levels are set to ensure that the quantities ordered do not tie up more capital than necessary.

If stock levels are to be monitored effectively, the records of stock movements must be accurate and kept up to date.

Stock Card Systems

A stock card system, or its computerised equivalent, is used for recording the movement of items in and out of stores. In order to ensure that supplies are always sufficient, the stock card should be updated every time stock is issued. At this time the amount stated as still held in stock can be checked against the minimum level. If these coincide, or nearly so, then a note can be kept or the need to reorder be indicated on the stock card according to the system used.

A convenient stock card system, both in regard to the updating of records and the ease of indicating the need to reorder, is the visible card system. This consists of cards with the name of the item typed on the bottom, together with any other information which needs to be seen at a glance. These cards are placed in overlapping pockets housed in metal trays. The pockets each have a transparent plastic shield, which allows information on the bottom of the card to be seen and also provides a carrier for coloured markers.

Markers are made in different materials, but particularly useful are the plastic ones which 'hook' under the bottom of the cards and hold firm. They are available in different colours so, for example, a marker of one colour can be used to indicate that items need to be reordered, and another of a different colour can be added to indicate that an order has been placed and delivery is awaited.

Stock cards in a system such as this can be written on without removing them from the pockets, thus saving time and retaining the continuity of the filing. Different coloured cards can be used to denote different categories of items in stock, thus speeding up recognition.

On the cards is written or typed the name of the item, plus a reference number if these are used. Also stated is the minimum stock level (the point at which an order is placed) and the maximum stock level. The quantity ordered should bring the amount in stock up to the maximum level.

The date, quantity received, invoice number and name of supplier is entered on the cards for goods in, and the date, quantity issued, requisition number and name of department entered for issues out. A running balance is kept so the amount in stock is known at all times (see Figure 5.2).

Stocks of specially printed items, such as letterheaded paper, need to have particular attention paid to them since they are expensive and can become out of date. As a safeguard, a coloured card, or some other type of marker, can be inserted between the packets of stock to indicate physically the minimum level.

Increasingly used are computer-based record keeping systems for maintaining stock records. Minimum and maximum levels are stored in the memory of the system. Receipts and issues are entered via the keyboard, the balance of stock is automatically updated and, if the minimum figure has been reached, the amount to be reordered is indicated. In more sophisticated systems the reordering process is automatically set in motion.

STATIONERY STOCK CARD

Item A4 Buff Bond Paper   **Ref. No.** BBP1

Maximum stock 85 reams   **Minimum stock** 25 reams

Date	Received			Issued			Balance in stock
	Quantity	Invoice No.	Supplier	Quantity	Requ. No.	Department	
6/7/19—				2 reams	81	Secretarial	30 reams
8/7/19—				5 reams	89	Sales	25 reams
18/7/19—				9 reams	102	Printing	16 reams
29/7/19—	60 reams	1496	Colorite Paper				76 reams
2/18/19—				2 reams	113	Secretarial	74 reams

Figure 5.2 Stationery stock card (if this were used in a visible card system, **Item** and **Ref** would appear at the bottom of the card)

Competence Builder 3

(Elements 3.3, 5.1)

a) In a real or simulated situation, demonstrate issuing stock items against requisitions, and updating records.

b) Assume that a minimum level has been reached after issuing one of the items requested. State what action you would take to replenish stocks.

c) If your organisation has a computerised stock system, ask to practise and/or demonstrate your ability to update records in a computerised database by:

▶ preparing and checking the data for input,
▶ entering the data using all necessary keys and commands,
▶ checking input data on the screen in order to detect and correct errors,
▶ searching a file for specified records.

Stocktaking

If records are kept accurately and care is taken in issuing goods, then the amounts shown in stock always equal the amounts actually held. However, there does need to be a physical count from time to time as a check against error. This is often done annually, so that it also provides the basis for a valuation of stock held for inclusion in the firm's accounts. More frequent stocktaking might be preferred, particularly for larger stores.

A perpetual inventory or continuous stocktaking method can also be adopted, whereby a certain number of items are checked each week. Stocktaking thus becomes part of the normal routine, saving the disruption of other work inevitably caused by an annual stocktake.

Computerised record keeping systems do not cut out the need for a physical count, but they do ease the valuation process. A complete statement of the balances of all stock in hand can be printed out, in some cases complete with values.

Competence Builder 4

(Element 5.1)

a) Under real or simulated conditions, carry out a sample stockcheck including the completion of stock inventory forms.

b) To whom should damages/discrepancies in stock be reported in your organisation?

Storage of Stock

A locked room or cupboard is usually set aside for the store. Ideally, this is conveniently placed for taking deliveries of goods into stock and for issuing items from stock. Access to the store and to the keys for it must be strictly controlled.

Storage must be arranged to ensure that goods are not damaged. Items must also be stored in such a way that difficulties do not arise when they are used. Paper, for example, can cause problems when used on machines if it is too damp or too dry.

Chemicals must be stored in accordance with regulations regarding them.

Safety must also be considered when deciding the height to which goods are stacked, and how they are reached.

The method of storage needs to be appropriate, for example small items should be kept neatly together in containers which allow them to be easily seen and easily reached.

Shelves should be clearly labelled. The size and distance between them needs to be sufficient for it to be easy to bring forward old stock and place new stock at the back. Strict rotation of stock helps to ensure that nothing is damaged. Paper in particular deteriorates with long storage.

The exact contents of packets should be stated on labels in order to avoid having to open the packets before it is necessary.

Housekeeping should be good – the store clean, tidy and dry, the floor clear, wrappers and boxes disposed of immediately they are empty and not left lying around.

Competence Builder 5   *(Elements 2.3, 5.1, 7.1)*

Find out if there are existing rules in your organisation regarding the care and storage of office consumables. If so make yourself a copy, preferably on a photocopier. If not prepare a notice regarding the care and storage of consumables which would be suitable for display where they are kept.

Receiving and Checking Deliveries

When goods are delivered they have to be checked for quantity and quality and any discrepancies must be reported. If goods are delivered by the supplier's own transport the driver has two copies of a delivery note. One copy is kept with the goods, the other is signed as a receipt and returned to the driver.

If at all possible goods should be inspected on delivery, but the practicality of this depends on their type and quantity. If it is not possible, then the copy of the delivery note returned to the driver must have added, when it is signed, a statement that the goods were received unchecked. The goods are later checked against the delivery note to ensure that what has been delivered is as stated. A check that there is no damage is also made at this stage.

Competence Builder 6 *(Elements 5.1, 9.1)*

Under real or simulated conditions:

a) Receive and check deliveries, store the goods and update the records.

b) Deal with an occasion when there is a discrepancy between the order and the goods supplied.

c) Deal with an item which requires careful or special handling and storage.

Efficiency and Economy

The efficiency of an office is considerably affected if consumables, and in particular stationery items, are not available when required. For this reason alone the systems adopted for stock control must be effective. They must also be cost-effective in regard to the use of staff time in carrying out duties connected with the care, control, issuing and ordering of stocks.

A good control system ensures that items are never out of stock. If this happens, it often results in a small quantity of the item having to be obtained as a stopgap at a considerably higher price than normal, for example forms might have to be photocopied at a greater cost than printing.

Stationery is a necessary cost of running a business, and a considerable one. Unfortunately the value of stationery is often disregarded in its use, and much unnecessary waste occurs.

Items should be used up completely – only one box of anything open at any one time, e.g. typewriter correction strips; only one bottle of anything open, e.g. correction fluid.

The right size and quality of an item should always be used. It is uneconomical, for example, to use paper, labels or envelopes larger or of a better quality than required for a particular job. This applies to many stationery items.

Anything that can be recycled should be: paper used on only one side can be reclaimed, stapled together and used for scrap pads; large envelopes can often be reused internally; file folders, wallets and binders can often be used again with a change of label.

Care taken by all members of staff helps to ensure that there is no unnecessary damage or waste. To a large extent this depends on their attitudes and awareness of the cost. The manner in which duties are carried out by those responsible for the storage, control and issue of stock can influence these attitudes and help staff to be cost-conscious.

Competence Builder 7   *(Element 5.1)*

For a period of time, say two weeks or a month, keep a note of any consumables you waste. Could any of this have been prevented? Could you have reclaimed anything wasted, for example paper for scrap pads? What is your organisation's policy on this?

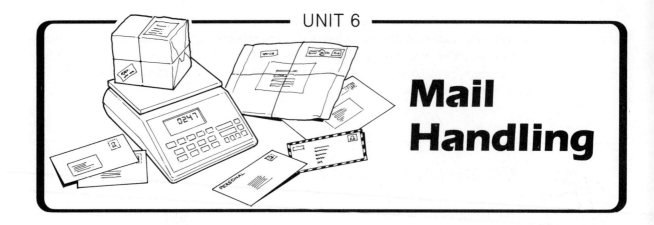

Mail Handling

In many large organisations, a central mailing department handles all the mail. This can be a full-time job for the people working in the department. Central mailing departments are usually well equipped with sophisticated machinery and time-saving devices to enable the staff to deal with large quantities of mail efficiently. In some cases the central mailing service is combined with central typing and reprographics. In small organisations, the 'mail' is only part of the work of one or more people.

As with other jobs on which the efficiency of an office depends, for example filing, many mailing tasks are routine. Unfortunately, this can devalue the work, its importance and cost, and allow problems arising through error to slip by. Error can result in unnecessary expense, breaches in security and confidentiality, and delays in dealing with urgent and important matters. Whatever the size of the mailing operation, it is important therefore that the established routine is strictly observed by all staff.

Competence Builder 1   *(Elements 3.1, 6.1, 6.2, 7.1)*

Find out about mail routines in your organisation. Write or type up notes for reference or photocopy existing instructions. Do these differ from those suggested in this unit? Are there reasons for this?

RECEIVING, SORTING AND DISTRIBUTING INCOMING MAIL

▶ The person receiving the mail is required to sign for any registered and recorded deliveries. The condition of all deliveries must then be checked for suspicious or dangerous items (see the section on security, p. 61), and any such items reported according to laid down procedures.

▶ Envelopes and packages marked 'personal', 'private' or 'confidential' are separated, date-stamped on the envelope and placed to one side to be passed unopened to the addressee.

▶ Packages are put aside for opening after the envelopes.

▶ Envelopes are stacked neatly, all facing the way that allows them to be opened in the most convenient manner. Thus a right-handed person using a paper knife should place the envelopes face downwards and slightly to the left. If a letter-opening machine is available, then the envelopes should be placed in such a way that will allow for the easiest feeding of them into the machine. Whatever the means used for opening the mail, this must be done carefully in order to avoid damage to the contents.

▶ After opening the envelopes, the contents are unfolded. Any enclosures are pinned together, with the correspondence on top. The actual enclosures are checked against those stated as being enclosed in the correspondence.

▶ Envelopes are rechecked to see that nothing has been left in them. If not too large in quantity they can be banded together and kept for a few days. This allows for the settling of any query which might require reference to a postmark. If there is too large a volume of mail, and/or rarely any queries, then it is best to dispose of the envelopes as soon as the mail has been dealt with.

▶ Every document is date-stamped – some stamps also include the time. It is more efficient to place the impression in the same place on each document. This also helps anyone checking the date. If papers are normally fastened together in a folder when filed (usually along the left-hand side), then they should be date-stamped on the right. The top corner is the place where people tend to notice things most readily.

▶ Money is generally entered in a remittances book after a check has been made that the amount received tallies with the amount stated in the correspondence. The opener's initials, plus a note of the amount and method of payment, are placed in a specified place on the correspondence (say under the date-stamp), as a proof of checking. The remittances are totalled and then passed to the cashier who signs for them.

▶ The correspondence is next sorted and distributed. If any needs to be dealt with by more than one person, then a choice has to be made: either a circulation slip, with the various parties' names on it, is attached; or photocopies are made for distribution to everyone. The latter has the advantage of passing on information more promptly, thus saving time if several matters have to be dealt with.

Whatever the procedure, mail should be passed on as soon as possible. It is helpful to place 'confidential' letters and those marked 'urgent' on top. Any unavoidable delays in distribution must be promptly reported to the appropriate person.

Competence Builder 2

(Elements 2.1, 6.1, 6.2)

a) In order to carry out mailing procedures successfully, it will be necessary for you to know the location and responsibilities of the people within your organisation. Check your knowledge of this and correct any deficiencies.

b) Draw up and keep a copy of a chart of your organisation showing the names and functions of the main departments.

c) Carry out incoming mail procedures under real or simulated conditions. You should deal with:

- ▶ items which are urgent, private or confidential,
- ▶ misdirected, registered or recorded delivery mail,
- ▶ mail with enclosures, and mail without all the stated enclosures,
- ▶ mail without the remittance enclosed,
- ▶ items not specifically addressed,
- ▶ packages.

Work to an already established time schedule or ask for one to be set. Self-check throughout.

PREPARING OUTGOING MAIL FOR DESPATCH

If there is a central mailing department, the staff from this usually collect mail from various points during the day or state deadlines for receiving it. These deadlines must be adhered to, but there are occasions when letters cannot be ready at the times stated. If such occasions are not too frequent they can probably be coped with. If frequent delays of mail cannot be avoided, then departmental secretaries usually keep a small supply of stamps and post letters personally.

Routines for dealing with outgoing mail are based on the following:

▶ Letters are checked for signature and attached enclosures before being inserted in the envelopes, at which time the addresses of letters and envelopes are checked to ensure that they tally. Any omissions and/or queries are reported or dealt with as appropriate.

▶ After sealing and packaging, the envelopes, packages and parcels are sorted into categories, for example first- and second-class letters, registered and recorded delivery mail, parcels, overseas mail. They are then weighed, and stamped or franked by machine.

▶ The envelopes are tied in bundles of the same category with all the addresses facing one way.

▶ Labels and forms for special items of mail, such as recorded delivery, are made out ready for receipting at the post office.

▶ Any necessary organisation records are completed ready for dealing with/ filing in accordance with laid down procedures.

▶ The mail is then ready for delivery to the post office. Arrangements can be made for large amounts to be collected.

Competence Builder 3 *(Elements 2.3, 6.2)*

a) Carry out outgoing mail procedures under real or simulated conditions. You should deal with a variety of items, including:

- ▶ letters with enclosures,
- ▶ parcels,
- ▶ recorded delivery and/or registered mail,
- ▶ Datapost.

Choose envelopes of appropriate size and ensure that they are sealed securely. Stamp or frank mail and record the postage total. Complete Post Office forms and any other records required. Check Post Office sorting requirements and postal deadlines in order to ensure that these are met. Appropriate reference books, for example the *Post Office Guide,* should be used. Deliver appropriate items to the post office and obtain the necessary receipts. Self-check throughout and follow security procedures for stamps and money at all times.

b) Double-check that you are using the mailroom equipment in your organisation safely. Ask for training on any equipment about which you are unsure.

c) Collect Post Office leaflets describing the postal services available. Keep these for reference.

d) Find out and keep a note of any services, other than those available from the Post Office, which offer express delivery or could meet other particular despatch requirements of your organisation.

SECURITY

Anyone handling mail will occasionally pick up information which, although not secret, is nevertheless not intended to be general knowledge. If ever you see any such information, you must therefore *not* discuss it. A recommended and frequently adopted procedure is for confidential letters to be inserted into their envelopes and sealed before they are sent out to the mailroom.

Mail containing remittances must be protected against theft, hence the need for records. Those coming in should be passed on as quickly as possible. Those going out, as indeed all mail, should be dealt with in such a way that they cannot be tampered with. Stamps must be kept locked away and be accounted for.

Letterbombs

Threats to security of a different nature arise from letterbombs. Anyone who opens mail needs to be on the alert for these. Examine letters and packets carefully, looking for anything unusual in the shape, thickness, size, weight and wrapping. Greasy marks, unusual smells, small holes or protruding wires are causes for suspicion. Anything strange about the writing or spelling are also matters for concern.

If suspicions are aroused, leave the packet where it is and do not open, squeeze, press or prod it or put it into anything. The room must be evacuated, locked and the key kept. The person responsible for safety and security in the organisation needs to be sent for, and/or the police, according to instructions laid down.

Competence Builder 4   *(Elements 2.3, 6.1, 6.2, 7.1, 9.1)*

a) Draw up a notice, suitable for display where the mail is dealt with, stating your organisation's instructions regarding security. *Or,* if photocopiable instructions exist, make a copy to keep.

b) Refer to Unit 9, Health and Safety. Make and keep a note of anything which particularly applies to working with the mail.

INTERNAL MAIL

This is frequently dealt with as part of the duties of those who handle the external mail. It operates in a variety of ways. In some organisations the internal mail is collected and distributed with the incoming mail. In others there are independent internal mail collections and deliveries throughout the day. Playing some part in the distribution of the internal mail is a good way to find out who and where people are in your organisation.

Competence Builder 5   *(Elements 6.1, 6.2)*

Find out how the internal mail system operates in your organisation. Ask to be shown the procedures for handling this. Arrange opportunities to carry them out for practice and later to prove your competence.

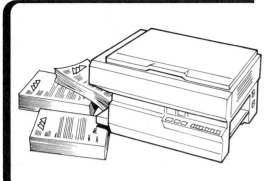

Reprographics

Information dealt with in an office often has to be filed in more than one place, or be read by more than one person. Also, the originator of a document usually needs to keep a copy for his or her own files. It is therefore necessary for some means of making additional copies of documents to be used.

PRODUCING COPIES FROM ORIGINAL DOCUMENTS

Photocopying is probably the most common of the various methods used for reproducing copies because of its convenience. The quality of the copies and the time taken to produce them depends on the type of copier. These factors will likely determine whether or not the copier is used to meet all the reprographic requirements of an organisation. Where large quantities of copies are frequently required, then duplicating methods are often used. The offset litho method in particular produces excellent quality copies.

Whatever the equipment, if you are to be competent in using it then you must be able to:

▶ start up, operate, and shut down the equipment, at all times following laid down operating and safety procedures,
▶ adjust the machine controls for quality and quantity, as appropriate,
▶ adjust the machine in order to produce enlarged and reduced size documents,
▶ produce copies which meet specified requirements, making minor permitted adjustments to the machine where this will improve quality,
▶ identify and reject copies which do not meet the standard required,
▶ cope with minor malfunctions of a machine by making permitted small adjustments,
▶ carry out routine cleaning, maintenance procedures and safety checks.

Carrying out these duties might mean that you have to read and interpret instruction manuals and you must therefore also be competent in doing this.

Competence Builder 1
(Elements 7.1, 9.1)

a) If you are unable to meet the requirements stated, then ask your boss or tutor for instruction on the reprographic equipment available in your organisation.

b) Find out the procedures to follow for reporting any malfunctions and/or break-down of the equipment, if you are not aware of this already.

Supplies and Records

You would find yourself very unpopular if you used reprographic equipment and then left it without the supplies of paper and other consumables that people following you might need. You should therefore find out from where to obtain these supplies, and always ensure that the equipment is well supplied after you have used it.

Correct storage of copier paper is important. It is useless if it becomes dirty or ragged, and can cause problems on the machine if it contains too much moisture. It should therefore always be kept wrapped until needed.

Many organisations require the completion of some form of record of use of the machine and you must be sure to fill this in. The equipment must not be used for personal copying unless there are special arrangements which permit this.

Recognising Competence

If you are competent in using your organisation's reprographic equipment you ought to be able to operate it with a minimum waste of material, even when using more advanced techniques such as copying back to back, copying onto letterheaded paper and, where the equipment permits, producing enlarged or reduced copies of the original. If there is some problem with the equipment you must be able to recognise this and identify the cause. Your competence will be judged against the following criteria:

▶ Copies meet specifications and are produced and correctly distributed, together with the original(s), within required deadlines.

▶ The wastage of materials is kept to a minimum.

▶ Unforeseen difficulties in achieving targets are promptly reported and the reasons politely explained.

▶ Faults are identified and dealt with in accordance with the manufacturer's instructions.

▶ Operating, recording and safety procedures are followed at all times.

Apart from operating the machine, you also need to be competent in communication skills. You must be able to interpret correctly oral and written instructions, plan and organise your work to meet deadlines (which might require some negotiation) and, as previously mentioned, complete any required records correctly and be able to read and interpret instruction manuals.

Competence Builder 2   *(Elements 3.1, 7.1)*

a) Negotiate with your boss or tutor opportunities for you to use the reprographic equipment available in your organisation in order to practise towards competence. When you consider that you can meet the criteria, ask for assessment.

b) Research the common reprographic methods available. Find out how copies are produced and how quickly, the quality obtainable and the cost per copy.

c) Find out what an operator of reprographic equipment needs to know about copyright law, and type a copy of this.

COLLATING AND FASTENING DOCUMENTS

Not only have copies to be made, they have also on occasions to be collated and fastened together. Some machines will collate as well as produce copies, and there is equipment available specifically for collating, but you might have to do this by hand. If so, then the most efficient way is to lay out your piles of pages in the following manner – the example is for a 12-page document. The same principles apply for more or fewer pages.

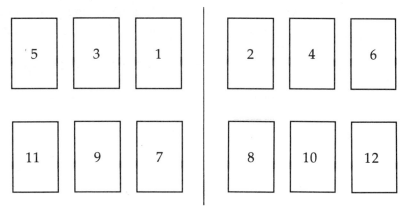

Figure 7.1

Using your left hand for collecting pages left of the line and your right hand for pages right of the line, pick up the pages in the following order: 12, 11, 10, 9, 8, 7, 6, 5, 4, 3, 2, 1.

You will then have the first page on the top and the other pages in order. You must make sure that you include a copy of each page in every set, so avoid doing this job where you might be distracted. You must also make sure that you pick up only one copy of each page at a time. Newly copied pages tend to stick together, so care is needed here.

The edges of the pages need to be brought into line after collating. This can be done by gently knocking the edges on the top of the desk or table, or by using the palm of your hand. If electric jogging equipment is available, then you might have the use of this.

You can then staple or bind the pages together by whatever means have been requested or are available. The job will be complete when you have filled in any necessary records, and distributed the copies and originals.

You must know and always follow safe practices in using equipment such as hand and automatic staplers and binders. You might be required to obtain supplies for these and must know how to do so. Where a task for assessment requires you to collate and fasten copies your competence will be judged by your results – i.e. that all pages are in the correct order and are neatly and securely fastened.

Competence Builder 3 *(Elements 2.3, 7.1)*

a) Ask your boss or tutor for opportunities to practise the skills involved in collating and fastening copies by carrying out the following activities when a suitable occasion arises:

▶ sorting, collating and straightening document pages,
▶ stapling/binding sets of documents,
▶ operating collating and binding equipment,
▶ completing the required records.

b) Look at a number of business equipment magazines – these might be available in your organisation or you could try the library – and make a list, with a brief description, of all the methods of fastening papers together that you can find. Your boss or tutor or your colleagues are alternative sources of information.

UNIT 8

Liaising with Callers and Colleagues

A major difference between business and personal life is that in business you cannot choose the people with whom you have to spend considerable amounts of time. If you are fortunate you will find that you can get along well with close colleagues, but it is unlikely that this will always be so. There will also undoubtedly be times when you have to liaise with callers to your office and organisation, and this will place you in a variety of situations where your competence in communicating and handling human relationships will be needed.

RECEIVING AND ASSISTING CALLERS

People visit your office or organisation for a number of different reasons. They come, for example, to impart information or to receive it, to discuss issues and projects and to complain. No matter what the reason for their visit is, you must always be courteous in receiving them. Callers, whether from outside or within the organisation, must always be greeted promptly using a form of greeting laid down or accepted by your organisation. Once you have established a person's name, continue to use it – this always makes a good impression.

Next you have to establish the reason for the visit. It sounds like a simple task, but is not always so. People are often not sure what they want or who they want to see, and even when they are sure do not always express their wishes clearly. In sorting this out you will find your listening and information interpreting skills useful, as well as the ability to ask appropriate questions.

You need to be very clear whether or not the caller has come about a matter with which you can personally deal. If not you must say so and request assistance from someone else. You need to know, therefore, on whom you can call, what the responsibilities of those people are, and where they can be found.

Competence Builder 1
(Elements 2.1, 2.2, 3.1, 7.1, 8.1, 8.2)

a) Find out to whom you should refer if you have any problems with a caller either through lack of knowledge or because the person is difficult in some way.

b) Find out about your organisation or, if it is a big one, that part of it where there are people with whom you have to liaise. Draw up a chart or diagram to show the names and positions of these people, as well as those that callers whom you have to receive are likely to wish to see. Include an outline of the main areas of work they deal with.

c) Find out if there are any internal directories or lists of internal telephone numbers. If there is a list of limited length, type a copy or make a photocopy of it.

d) Ask your boss or tutor to check your competence in making internal telephone calls, both in using the equipment and your telephone manner. (Refer to Unit 2.)

There might be occasions when callers have to wait in order to be seen by some other person. When this happens, apologise to the caller for the delay and, where possible, give some indication of how long this might be. Depending on what is usual in your organisation, you can then offer to hang up the caller's coat or hat, offer a magazine or newspaper, and a cup of tea or coffee.

There will be occasions when callers either cannot be seen or they have not time to wait. In such cases you might be asked to take a message (see Unit 2).

Competence Builder 2
(Elements 2.2, 8.1)

In a real situation or in role play, deal with the following:

a) a caller with a query who is not very good at stating what this is, and who does not know whom to ask for in the organisation,

b) a caller who is going to have to wait to be seen,

c) a caller who wishes to leave a message,

d) an aggressive caller with a complaint.

Security

Callers to an organisation are usually asked to sign a book or some other form of log recording their visit. This not only provides a permanent record of callers but also shows who is on the premises in the event of an emergency. For this latter reason people are often asked to sign out as well as in. They may also be given a badge, which they should be asked to wear in such a way that it can be seen. For reasons of safety, anyone who has anything to do with callers must make sure that briefcases, or anything else carried in, are not left where others can fall over them. You must also make sure, because this has been used as a method for planting bombs, that briefcases leave with callers.

Security of information is also important, and the requirements which have to be met will be governed by the work of the organisation. Because of this there are variations in the degree of freedom within a building that is allowed to callers. In some organisations a commissionaire will escort callers, in others they will be asked to make their own way to the office of the person expecting them. In others you might be expected to escort the caller.

If you do have to escort callers to some other part of the building, it is usual for social pleasantries to be exchanged during the walk. You might ask questions such as 'Did you have any trouble in finding us?', make some remark about parking, or fall back on that perennial favourite, the weather. It is important that you resist discussing the activities of the organisation or of any of its staff. It is not uncommon for staff to be actively 'pumped' by callers for such information. If you ever find yourself in this situation, simply plead ignorance of the matters being questioned.

Competence Builder 3   (Element 8.1)

Unless you are already certain about them, find out about the security rules in your organisation in regard to callers. Make sure that you always abide by them.

If you have to escort a caller to an office, you might be called upon to make a formal introduction. If so, announce the caller's name, title and organisation clearly, following the rule of introducing men to women, juniors to seniors, and everyone to VIPs. If a caller is known, you simply announce 'Mr Green to see you'. Under no circumstances should you show a caller into an office unannounced, or escort a caller to someone's office without first establishing that it is alright to do so.

If you have to leave a caller alone by your desk at any time it is wise to slip into a drawer or folder any documents which are lying around. A stranger or indeed an unauthorised member of staff, should never have ready access to information which might be of commercial advantage to them. This includes a much wider range of papers than those acknowledged as confidential, so it is best to be cautious.

Competence Builder 4   (Elements 8.1, 9.1)

In a real situation and/or in role play, deal with the following:

a) a caller who presses for information which cannot be disclosed,

b) a caller who is about to leave without his or her belongings,

c) a caller who tries to avoid signing in,

d) a caller who tries to go somewhere unescorted, or some place where access is restricted,

e) a caller who causes a safety hazard, e.g. places a briefcase where someone might fall over it.

MAINTAINING BUSINESS RELATIONSHIPS WITH OTHER MEMBERS OF STAFF

The people with whom you work may come from differing backgrounds and have differing ideas and viewpoints. Do not let such differences become barriers, it is essential to get on with work colleagues. You have to rely on one another for help and advice and have to co-operate in many ways.

If you respond willingly to requests from colleagues, they will more likely respond similarly to you. When requests cannot be met, explain why not clearly and politely, in the hope that colleagues will behave in the same way when they cannot meet your requests. If you establish a good rapport from the beginning, you should expect to be able to discuss difficulties in working relationships, and this is the first step towards resolving them. If difficulties arise which cannot be resolved, then these must be referred to someone in higher authority. They should not be allowed to continue, because the situation is likely to deteriorate rather than improve.

Being discreet is important and it is wise to refuse to listen to or repeat office gossip, scandal and rumour, or indulge in time-wasting chit chat. Being tactful, friendly and cheerful, showing that you have common sense and can be relied on to maintain a sense of humour are always good characteristics to display.

Trust is important in a number of ways. You have to trust your colleagues and they in turn have to trust you. Your organisation has to trust you not to discuss matters regarding work with others who are not entitled to such information. If you know what work other members of staff do, then it is far easier to decide whether or not to pass on information or refer the matter to your boss.

Competence Builder 5   *(Elements 2.3, 7.1, 8.2)*

a) Make a photocopy of the chart you produced in Competence Builder 1b). Tick those people to whom you would give information without question. Circle those whose requests you would refer to your boss or tutor.

b) If you are employed, decide what areas of your work you should regard as confidential and not to be discussed without authorisation. Check this with your boss.

The Boss

Bosses differ! Some are considerate and informative, and will offer a helpful word now and again. Others will leave you to 'get on with it'. However much or little help you are given, it is always best to cover yourself. Check anything which is not clear and make notes for reference if you are in doubt. If you make a mistake, apologise and ask to be shown again. Needing help, provided it is not too frequently, can often be better than appearing to 'know it all'.

The following helpful hints checklist will help in maintaining good business relationships, particularly with the boss:

▶ Organise your routine jobs so that the best use is made of the time available.

▶ Try to get work done to time, avoiding the temptation to leave jobs you do not like.

▶ Always be punctual – no one likes to be kept waiting.

▶ Keep to a minimum any time taken off for personal reasons.

▶ Keep office machines clean, and use covers where provided.

▶ Don't let up on improving the speed and accuracy of your work – the latter is very important.

▶ If responsible for supplies of stationery, make sure there is always plenty available. It is embarrassing to give lack of stationery as a reason for not doing a job or, worse, prevent someone else from doing their work.

▶ Ensure that all your work is neat, and pay particular attention to spelling and punctuation.

▶ Always check numbers, names and addresses, and dates.

▶ Listen carefully to instructions in order to avoid error, or the necessity of having to ask for them to be repeated.

▶ Maintain a tidy workplace with personal belongings out of sight, and desk, equipment and cupboards neat.

▶ Be reliable – both in carrying out tasks and in conveying information.

▶ Be quiet – in conversation, in closing doors, in using equipment and in general movement around the office.

▶ Always carry a notebook and pencil when going to see someone who might give instructions or information. Things written down are less likely to be forgotten.

Competence Builder 6   (Elements 7.1, 8.2)

Photocopy the helpful hints checklist. Tick those items relevant to your situation in training, at college or at work. How do you match up? Where is there room for improvement? Underline these. Set yourself realistic dates for meeting the items underlined.

OFFICE DRESS

Convention in what is regarded as acceptable office dress has changed greatly during the past few years and a fairly informal mode of dress is generally regarded as quite acceptable. Nevertheless, in any one organisation the degree of informality will depend on the type of business and the preference of the management. If you have to meet at work people from outside the organisation, then it is most important that you wear appropriate clothes at all times. Being competent and well organised is not enough; you must look the part as well.

Your clothes should always be clean, fresh and unstained. They should fit well and accessories should blend in. Limit the amount of jewellery, avoiding anything which rattles or jangles. The noise can become irritating to others who are trying to concentrate. Give consideration also to safety aspects – long beads, chains and bracelets can catch on handles and other moving parts of office machinery.

If your clothes are smart and attractive, you can change the accessories or make other slight adjustments to dress them up for an afterwork date when there is not time to go home to change. It is surprising how much walking about you can do in an office so take time in choosing shoes in order to ensure that they are not only good looking but will also be comfortable to wear for long periods.

Other things to pay attention to are: for women carefully applied moderate make-up, for men closely shaved or tidily trimmed facial hair; well cared for hands and skin; thorough personal hygiene; well brushed clean hair arranged in an attractive style; a good posture and graceful movements. Perfumes and aftershave are fine in moderation, but too much can be overpowering. A light cologne is safer than a headier fragrance.

Your choice of clothing should also fit in with your working environment and work duties. There is often an accepted mode of dress. If you worked in a law firm, for example, you would expect to dress differently from how you would dress if you worked in the beauty or leisure fields. Whether it be glamorous or casual, your image must be appropriate.

Competence Builder 7
(Elements 8.1, 8.2)

Critically assess your business image. Better still, ask a friend or a colleague whom you can trust to offer constructive criticism. Can you make improvements?

UNIT 9

Health and Safety

Safety starts with you. You must always take care in regard to your own health and safety and also that of any other person working with you or who may be affected by what you do. You must also co-operate with your employer, or any other person with responsibility for seeing that health and safety functions are carried out, by:

▶ following laid down routine safety procedures and practices,
▶ taking appropriate action when hazardous and potentially hazardous situations arise,
▶ following laid down procedures in the event of fire, accident or other emergency,
▶ keeping your own work area tidy and free from hazards.

There are certain Acts of Parliament which particularly affect workers in business administration. These are the Offices, Shops and Railway Premises Act 1963, and the Health and Safety at Work Act 1974.

OFFICES, SHOPS AND RAILWAY PREMISES ACT

This act lays down minimum requirements of employers in regard to the physical working conditions of their employees. Employers are required to meet stated standards on matters such as cleanliness, sufficient working space and suitable seating, heating and ventilation, lighting, toilets and washing facilities, the provision of drinking water, and arrangements for hanging up and drying clothes. Fire precautions, safety measures and the provision of first aid boxes are also covered.

Competence Builder 1
(Element 9.1)

Find out and keep a note of the aspects of the Offices, Shops and Railway Premises Act which are relevant to work in an office.

74

HEALTH AND SAFETY AT WORK ACT

Often referred to by its initials, HASAWA, this act is significant in that it lays a responsibility on employees as well as employers for ensuring that the workplace is safe and that people are protected.

> It shall be the duty of every employee to take reasonable care for the health and safety of himself and of other persons who may be affected by his acts or omissions at work.

In practical terms this means being generally aware of safety – not being careless, lazy, overconfident or impatient – and being well informed regarding potential dangers and the safety rules and emergency procedures to follow.

Competence Builder 2   (Elements 3.1, 9.1)

a) Type up notes for reference, stating in your own words the general obligations of employers, employees and members of the public in regard to the Health and Safety at Work Act.

b) Identify the location of fire alarms in the building in which you work or study and find out the names of the organisation's safety representatives.

OPERATING SAFELY IN THE WORKPLACE

An office is a considerably more hazardous workplace than people generally realise. The rest of this unit looks at common sources of injury and provides guidelines on how to make the office safer.

Collision, and Unsafe Use of Office 'Furniture'

▶ Always approach doors on the side away from the hinges. This allows you, or anyone you are about to meet in the doorway, to step to one side. Make sure you know where there are any clear glass doors, and look out for them when you are in unfamiliar locations. This will help to avoid collision with them.

▶ Fill bottom filing cabinet drawers first and avoid overloading top drawers to ensure that the cabinet does not topple over. Some cabinets are made in such a way that it is impossible to open more than one drawer at the same time. Where this is not so, then open one only at a time to avoid causing the cabinet to fall forward. Make sure that drawers are completely closed – heads can be banged against upper ones, bottom ones fallen over. Close drawers carefully, using the handles, to avoid trapping your fingers. Do not tug when a drawer is difficult to open. If it opened suddenly you might fall over; also the action of bending down and pulling can cause back damage.

▶ Avoid overloading lateral filing cabinets and shelves, they easily tip over. Heavy or breakable items are best stored on bottom shelves, frequently used ones where they are easily reached. Nothing should be stored on the top of the cabinet. Using a secure stepladder or stool is the safest way of reaching items which are stored high. Never use a swivel chair for this purpose.

Competence Builder 3   *(Elements 1.1, 1.2, 9.1)*

Demonstrate to your boss or tutor the correct use of filing cabinets and shelves. Always use these methods as a matter of course.

Machinery, Equipment and Stationery

▶ First learn how to operate machinery correctly and safely. Turn off and unplug machines before adjusting or repairing them, and do not attempt adjustments or repairs of any kind unless you are authorised and trained to do so. Any machine that appears abnormal – that is it overheats, sparks, smokes or causes shocks – should be turned off, unplugged and reported. Any frayed or bare wires, overloaded outlets or improperly grounded wires should also be reported. Machines not in use are safest when switched off. Dangerous machinery such as guillotines must be fitted with guards.

▶ Take particular care in handling the chemicals used in machines. Avoid physical contact by using gloves and an apron. Wash your hands when you have finished. Many correcting and cleaning fluids give off an inflammable vapour. Replace tops immediately after use. Use a locked, well ventilated cupboard for storing such materials.

▶ Avoid dangling jewellery, scarves, belts, loose sleeves and ties. They are potentially dangerous if you wear them when using machinery with exposed moving parts. It is wise to consider this when dressing for the office.

▶ Place equipment securely on desks and make sure that there are no parts overhanging.

▶ Do not mix drawing pins with paper clips. Store scissors and other pointed or sharp objects where they can be seen when being taken out.

▶ Disinfect ear plugs used for audio equipment before and after use to ensure a high standard of hygiene. Anything of this nature should ideally be kept on a personal basis.

▶ Handle paper items in such a way that cuts are avoided. Using finger guards and moistening stamps and envelopes with a sponge or similar are good precautions to take. Use paper cutters carefully: do not cut too many sheets at a time and keep your fingers well away from the blade.

Competence Builder 4 *(Elements 3.1, 9.1)*

a) Check that your own work area is tidy and free from hazards.

b) Type up and keep a list of do's and don'ts to serve as a personal reminder to follow tidy, safe and hygienic working practices.

c) Check your knowledge regarding the safe operation and care of the equipment and machinery you use. Ask for training in anything about which you are uncertain.

Falling, Slipping and Tripping

These are common accidents and can arise in a number of different ways. Take the following precautions:

▶ Make sure that lighting is sufficient and try not to work anywhere where it is not.

▶ Wear 'sensible' shoes and not ones with heels which are difficult to walk on or which might get stuck in something and throw you forward.

▶ Pick up or wipe up anything which might cause a slip.

▶ Use the handrails on stairs, take steps one at a time, and report any damage to them.

▶ Do not carry loads which you cannot see over.

▶ Watch out for loose or damaged floor surfaces, and recently washed or waxed floors.

▶ Keep gangways free of personal belongings which someone might trip over.

▶ Do not leave flex trailing from a socket to a piece of equipment.

▶ Do not tilt back in a chair. Chairs can overbalance, or become damaged so that they may break and hurt someone.

Competence Builder 5 *(Elements 8.2, 9.1)*

a) Carry out a general survey in the building identifying any health and safety hazards. Discuss with your boss or tutor how these might best be brought to the attention of the relevant person.

b) Carry out a detailed survey of the area immediately surrounding where you work or study. Carry out any improvements for which you do not need to seek approval. Discuss other possible improvements with your boss or tutor.

Using VDUs, Keyboarding and Good Posture

If you use a VDU (visual display unit), take precautions to minimise eyestrain. This can be accomplished in a number of ways:

▶ Avoid placing the VDU where lights are reflected in the screen.

▶ Adjust blinds or the angle of the screen to minimise glare.

▶ Use lighting specially designed for VDU operation.

▶ Use the brightness control on the machine to suit the conditions.

▶ Keep the screen clean and fingermark free.

▶ Have your eyes tested regularly and advise your optician of the nature of the work you do.

When using a VDU or other keyboard, reduce fatigue by:

▶ wherever possible varying your routine to avoid boredom and increase your physical movement,

▶ adjusting the height of your chair and backrest to achieve the most comfortable position,

▶ sitting up straight and well back on your chair,

▶ keeping your feet flat on the floor, using a footrest if necessary,

▶ supporting your thighs on the chair.

Competence Builder 6   *(Elements 3.1, 9.1)*

When using a VDU, check the conditions under which you have to operate it. Can you personally minimise eyestrain and fatigue in any of the ways suggested? Negotiate with your boss or tutor other possible improvements.

Lifting

Incorrect lifting and carrying of very heavy objects are potential sources of damage to the body which can remain for the rest of your life. Heavy machines or other objects should be moved using a trolley. Where something can reasonably be carried, and it has to be lifted first, there is a recognised way of doing so which avoids back injury. Practise this and then follow the same procedure at all times:

▶ Stand facing and close to the item to be lifted with your feet apart for balance.

▶ Squat down keeping your back straight and bending your knees.

▶ Grasp whatever is to be lifted firmly.

▶ Breathe in deeply.

▶ Lift slowly, straightening your legs and returning your back to the vertical position.

▶ Hold the item you are carrying firmly and close to your body.

Competence Builder 7   (Element 9.1)

Demonstrate to your boss or tutor, on a number of items of office equipment, the correct techniques for lifting and carrying.

Fire

▶ Even if you are allowed to do so, avoid smoking in the office, storerooms or wherever there could be a fire risk.

▶ If you are a smoker, always use ashtrays, or other recognised receptacles, and *not* wastebins.

▶ Store properly all materials which are flammable.

▶ Store and dispose of rags, or any other materials which might be fire hazards, in an agreed manner.

▶ Use stoves, or other appliances provided for making refreshments, with caution and ensure that they are turned off after use.

▶ Do not overload electrical circuits.

▶ Be familiar with evacuation procedures. Make sure that you know the exit to make for and the place where people have to go when they leave the building.

▶ If a fire occurs, get out of the building quickly and never use a lift.

▶ Know the organisation's policy for reporting a fire and carry this out if it becomes necessary to do so.

Competence Builder 8

(Elements 2.3, 9.1)

a) Draw up and keep a copy of a safety notice stating the correct sequential procedure to adopt in the event of an accident, fire or other emergency.

b) Locate alarms, first aider, first aid equipment and fire fighting equipment in your own work area.

c) Find out the main causes of fire in an office and the type of fire extinguisher appropriate to use in each case.

d) Discuss with your boss or tutor an accident or emergency situation realistic to your work or study situation. Suggest appropriate action to take if this occurred. If you are a student or trainee, role play this as a group.

e) Complete and keep a copy of an accident report form after establishing with your boss or tutor appropriate information regarding an imaginary accident, or one which occurred at some previous time. This could be a follow-up on d).

You can make a positive contribution to your own health and safety, and that of the people with whom you work or study, if you are careful and take time to do things in the recommended ways. If you are in any doubt about safety rules or what to do in an emergency, ask your boss or tutor *now*.

Part II

Building Your Job Seeking Competences

Job Seeking

The very act of seeking a job gives you an opportunity to demonstrate valued abilities such as initiative, perseverance, the ability to cope with the unexpected, information seeking and communication skills. It is an opportunity which should be exploited. Everything, from the first contact on, can influence a prospective employer when deciding whether or not to offer the job to you.

FINDING A VACANCY

Giving your undivided attention to job seeking is likely to bring the quickest results. It is too time-consuming to write after one or two jobs and then sit back awaiting replies. You should explore all avenues at the same time. Not only is this quicker, but it is easier to cope with any rejections when you have other possibilities in hand.

In addition to exploring the more usual job sources (which follow), you should scan the local newspapers for reports such as those stating that an organisation is expanding. Following these up to see if the expansion is likely to mean the possibility of a job is a long shot, but initiative and enterprise is valued and for the price of a letter or telephone call you may be lucky.

Careers Service

You are probably already familiar with the careers service. It is an organisation which caters specifically for the under 18s and covers most school and many college leavers. Its staff usually go into these establishments on a regular basis. The emphasis is very much on careers advice, which is free and freely given. You can therefore expect to get much more from the service than just the name of a firm to which you can apply for a job.

Jobcentres

Jobcentres are primarily for the over 18s and at these also the service is entirely free. Although the staff will advise people under 18, first appointments and notification of jobs for the younger age group usually go to the careers service. Jobcentres were set up to provide a 'shop window' for jobs, and advertisements are displayed on a self-selection basis. Beyond this, anyone requiring advice can request an interview and/or ask to be notified in the event of a suitable job arising.

Employment Agencies

Employment agencies are listed in the *Yellow Pages* telephone directory and are more numerous in the larger cities. They generally operate by charging a fee to the employer, not to the applicant, and are useful to the employer in 'screening' applicants. Their interviews are similar to a job interview, and you should take along documents such as references and curriculum vitae when you apply. The agency registers applicants and will send them for any suitable jobs immediately available and any which arise subsequently.

Advertisements

Jobs are advertised in trade journals and newspapers, both as display and small advertisements. Read them carefully, because if a particular type or length of experience is specified the firm is unlikely to be interested in anyone not meeting that specification – unless of course the vacancy is in an area where clerical staff are in short supply. If, however, the advertisement asks for a typewriting speed slightly higher than what you can offer, it is still worth applying in the hope of impressing the firm with your other qualities or qualifications. After all, speed can be increased with practice.

Direct Applications and Recommendations

The majority of jobs are never advertised. This is a fact to exploit. Some large firms and organisations such as the Civil Service employ so many people it is always worth contacting them to find out if there is a vacancy. Similarly, organisations to which you are particularly attracted are worth approaching. In this case, state definite reasons for your application and not just a 'liking' for the firm. End such an enquiry with a request to be advised in the event of a vacancy arising later if there is nothing currently available.

Knowing someone who knows someone is an effective way of getting a job. Many firms advise employees of vacancies. Friends and relatives can be useful in this respect, so make sure they all know what it is you are looking for. A personal recommendation will not automatically lead to a job offer but it can help, especially if it comes from an employee who is well thought of.

Competence Builder 1 *(Element 2.3)*

If you are currently job seeking (or when you are), think about and make a list of the qualities and abilities you have, and those you could improve or develop. Match these up with those which seem to be needed for any jobs you consider applying for. If you have a choice, apply for jobs which would use the qualities and abilities you already have. Thinking carefully about what you can offer will help you to put yourself forward in the best possible light.

APPLYING FOR A VACANCY

Almost without exception everyone who applies for a job has to make some sort of written application. This might take the form of a letter incorporating all the necessary details, or a short letter accompanied by a curriculum vitae. A printed application form is often provided.

Whatever the nature of the application it is usually the first detailed contact between applicant and prospective employer, and as such is very important. Since its aim is to secure an interview, it is essential that it makes a good impression on the mind of the person shortlisting applicants. It is an opportunity to sell yourself and to promote the impression of being the most suitable applicant. Emphasise any particularly relevant abilities and qualifications. In doing this, always be truthful. If your application is successful it will go on file and could be an embarrassment during your employment if it is inaccurate. It also usually provides a basis for questions asked during interview, when you will be asked to substantiate statements you have made or to speak about them in more detail.

You should always find out as much as you can about the organisation to which you are applying. If you can weave this knowledge into the application it will convey an impression of interest. If you already have working experience, emphasise any special contributions this would enable you to make. Indicate any links between previous experience and the post you are applying for.

Letters of Application

Presentation is of the utmost importance. If you are applying for a post which includes typing duties, then you must send a typewritten letter (unless the advertisement specifies 'in own handwriting') set out in an orthodox manner, written in good English and free from spelling and punctuation errors. Corrections should not be detectable. Nothing less than sheer excellence will do. Word the letter in a businesslike manner. Use your usual signature and, although this should be legible, type your name under the signature.

In most cases there are a number of people applying for any one job, so the employer has plenty of choice. Applications containing a mass of irrelevant information are likely to be placed on the rejection pile. Your letter should therefore be brief, whilst at the same time incorporating all the necessary information. Make sure you refer to the specific job you are applying for, since the firm might have several vacancies at the same time. It is an irritating waste of time for a prospective employer to have to search for some clue as to which vacancy is being applied for, and the rejection pile might be a tempting alternative!

Use simple, straightforward language, avoiding long words where shorter ones will do equally well. Phrases such as 'await the favour of your reply' are old-fashioned: leave them out. Do not use slang or abbreviations such as 'advert' instead of advertisement, or 'thanks' instead of thank you.

Competence Builder 2   *(Elements 2.3, 2.4, 3.1)*

Type a letter of application for real or for practice. If the latter, base it on a job advertisement which you can attach to the letter and place in your personal file for future reference.

Curriculum Vitae

In order to determine a shortlist of applicants to interview, an employer has to take a good look at what each candidate has to offer to see how this matches up with what the job requires. Such details are usually set out in a curriculum vitae (CV), which is attached to a short letter of application.

In preparing a CV you begin with a short list of details about yourself, including your name, address, telephone number and date of birth. Follow this, under the heading 'Education', with details of the schools and colleges you attended, in chronological order with dates. Details of any vocational training can be shown here also – in which case the heading should read 'Education and Training'. Alternatively, you could include 'Training' as a separate heading. State qualifications under a separate heading or include them under 'Education and Training'.

'Employment Experience' (if any) should follow, including a brief outline of duties as well as a job title. This list should be in chronological order.

Any additional information you consider relevant, for example special skills and interests, follows next. The final item is that of 'References', at which point you give the names, addresses and telephone numbers of two people, or more if requested. The people you give as referees must have agreed to this. It is difficult to know whom to ask when applying for a first job. School head teachers, college principals or heads of department are appropriate people, as are people whom you have known for a long period of time.

There are no fixed rules regarding layout, but it is important that your CV is easy to read. A simple example is shown in Figure 10.1. It is useful to type at the top your name, the date, and the job you are applying for, as a safeguard in case the CV becomes separated from your letter of application.

```
CURRICULUM VITAE

Emily MATTHEWS
7 Greenley Road, Birmingham, SH7 6PG
Telephone 021-701-7314

Date of birth    14 March 1972

Education        September 1982 – July 1988
                 Long Stream Comprehensive

Training         July 1988 - July 1990
                 Youth Training at Officewise

Qualifications   GCSE: English; Maths; C & G Business Administration
                 Level 2

References        Mr G R Dobson MA             Mr R Max
                  Principal                    General Manager
                  Long Stream Comprehensive    Officewise
                  Cookson Lane                 Green End
                  Shirley                      Shirley
                  Birmingham SH6 8PD           Birmingham SH6 5L0
                  Tel. no. 021-701-8902        Tel. no. 021-701-6253
```

Figure 10.1 Curriculum vitae

Competence Builder 3 *(Elements 2.3, 3.1)*

If you have not prepared a CV, do so now. If you have one already, then criticise it constructively and revise it if necessary.

Application Forms

Many employers provide application forms, and completing these can on the surface appear preferable to writing a letter. However, they are not always as straightforward as they might at first appear.

Instructions, sometimes small and tucked away, need to be followed carefully. You will create a bad impression immediately if, for instance, you fail to use block capitals where asked to do so, or if, on discovering the error, you then scribble out the original entry. With this in mind, it makes good sense to read the form thoroughly before you start to complete it. This also allows you to make any decisions as to the most appropriate place for putting the various items of information – there might be alternatives.

Drafting the answers on a piece of paper, or better still on a photocopy of the form, helps further to avoid alterations on the form. Always read the draft through critically yourself and, if possible, get someone else to do so as well.

All details should be accurate and as full as possible. Application forms are no place for excessive modesty. Distinctiveness is desirable but difficult to achieve. Forms are deliberately designed to present a standardised picture of applicants so that they can be compared more easily. Additional points can be added on a separate sheet, but you have to be wary of overkill.

Filling in application forms is demanding, time-consuming work, but is the key to opening interview doors. Answer all questions, or state 'not applicable' where appropriate. This is important since it indicates that you have not missed the question or omitted an answer in error.

Forms look better when completed on the typewriter, but check first that this is feasible. Many form designers fail to lay out forms in such a way that there is adequate space or that horizontal rulings correspond with the line spacing on a typewriter. If a form is difficult but possible to complete on the typewriter, and you can do it well, then this is bound to gain points where the post requires typewriting skills.

Always keep copies of letters and completed application forms. If you are called for interview, these can be referred to as a check as to what you have already said. They are also useful for reference and save time when you apply for other jobs.

Competence Builder 4   (Elements 2.3, 3.1)

If you will be applying for jobs involving typewriting, then practise completing forms (preferably application forms, but others will do) on the typewriter. The better you are able to do this, the more skilful you will show yourself to be without actually having to say so!

Telephone Applications

If a company needs to select someone quickly, or wishes to assess their telephone manner, then initial application by telephone might be requested. This can be an advantage in that it usually avoids the need for a letter of application, and the invitation for interview may be made immediately.

You should observe all the important rules about making telephone calls in these cases, particularly in regard to knowing who to ask for and having all details to hand. Such calls can take quite some time, so it is best to avoid using a phone box.

Start the conversation by announcing your name, the job you are applying for, and stating where your information regarding the vacancy came from. Give your personal details sufficiently slowly to allow for notes to be taken. Having paper and pencil yourself is essential for similarly jotting down any information given. If an invitation to attend for interview results from the telephone conversation, then confirm your acceptance immediately by letter.

Competence Builder 5 *(Element 2.3)*

Select an advertisement for a job you would like and jot down notes you could use if applying for it by telephone.

There is one very important quality in applying for a job – enthusiasm. This should be evident throughout all the negotiations. No one is going to be keen to offer you a job if you do not sound really interested in it.

Making the Most of the Interview

The interview is frequently thought of as an opportunity for the employer to compare shortlisted applicants on a face-to-face basis. It is more than this. It is a two-way process, an opportunity to exchange information: for the interviewer to ask for items in the application to be clarified or enlarged upon; for the applicant to ask questions and decide if in fact the job would suit.

Employers usually have many applications for a vacancy, but making the right choice is not easy. They are looking for a person who will carry out the duties of the post as they wish, yet all they have to base their decision on is the application and the interview.

Mistakes in selection are costly for the employer: the law is strict regarding dismissal and the processes involved in filling a vacancy are expensive. It is equally costly for you to accept a job which proves not to have been a good choice. You might have passed up other opportunities, and trying several jobs can lead to a future prospective employer thinking you have no interest in work or no stickability. Also, since you will spend many hours at work, you should expect to derive some pleasure and satisfaction from them.

PREPARING FOR THE INTERVIEW

The interview is the final hurdle in securing the right job, and it therefore needs to be carefully prepared for. This includes thinking about the image you wish to present and the questions you will want to ask.

Appearance

What to wear? What impression to give? Certainly not that of dropping in on the way to a party, or of having been interrupted in the middle of a physically demanding chore. Although dress for the office is far less formal today than it was just a few years ago, it is nevertheless still fairly conventional. In some lines of business, and for some employers, it is still extremely conventional. It is possible to indicate by your appearance that you are efficient and prepared to work hard. Obviously casual clothes will not do this.

Men will generally be expected to wear a shirt and tie rather than a sweater or T-shirt, and to wear a jacket. Women can always be sure of being dressed acceptably if they wear a skirt (provided this is not too short). It is best to avoid revealing necklines and not to overdo make-up. Both sexes should avoid extremes in hair fashion and over-bright clothes. A further danger to avoid is deliberately 'dressing up' – if this means wearing unfamiliar clothing which you feel conscious about or have to adjust in some way.

Feeling confident in looking your best and conveying a businesslike image are the twin aims of interview dressing. No matter how good your application, the interviewer is likely to be influenced by your appearance – and remember that this is not just to do with clothes and physical attributes. It is equally to do with the way you walk, sit, and make use of facial expressions. A lack of self-consciousness and a pleasant smile also make an important contribution (see also Unit 8).

Competence Builder 1 *(Elements 8.1, 8.2)*

Imagine you are going for a job interview tomorrow. Which of your clothes will you wear? Include accessories and jewellery. Could you improve on this presentation of yourself? If so, how? What can you do to effect these improvements?

Before the Interview

Part of your preparation for the interview should include thinking about what questions you could ask in order to find out more information about the firm. There is usually an opportunity, during an interview or at the end, for you to ask questions or make some comment. To do so is better than sitting dumb. It is also an opportunity to make a favourable impression in a manner that might not have arisen before. Questions about the job itself, for example further prospects and training, are more likely to impress than a question about how much holiday there will be. It is a good plan to jot down a few questions on a card which you can then pop into a pocket or bag and produce at an appropriate time. You should also take the letter inviting you to attend for interview and any certificates you might need as proof of your qualifications.

Competence Builder 2 *(Element 2.3)*

Take an advertisement for a job which you are going to, or could, apply for. Make a list of questions you would want to ask at an interview. Discuss these with your fellow students or trainees, as appropriate.

You should have kept a copy of your application. Check through this shortly before the interview. The interviewer will almost certainly wish to pick up points from this and ask for clarification or elaboration on the information you gave. If you have already rehearsed the answers to possible questions, you will be able to give more confident responses.

Interviews for jobs involving typing often include a test and you should take some means of making corrections. In such a test, accuracy is more important than speed. The employer will be aware that a higher speed is likely in a more relaxed atmosphere and, especially for a first job applicant, speed will increase with confidence and experience.

Go to bed early the night before the interview. No amount of preparation can alleviate a feeling of being jaded and tired, or the difficulty of answering questions in such a condition.

THE INTERVIEW

Arriving in good time without having had to rush will help you to feel calm and efficient. Allow plenty of time for the journey, bearing in mind possible delays and hold-ups. Find out exactly where to go, how to get there and how long it will take. Aiming to arrive a little earlier than called for will leave you a few minutes for any necessary freshening up.

When you arrive, the first person you are likely to see is the receptionist to whom you give your name and information regarding the appointment. The receptionist will show you where you can leave items such as a coat or umbrella (ask, if necessary), which will save you wondering what to do with them in the interview room.

While you are waiting, it is useful to try and absorb some of the 'atmosphere' of the place if only to take your mind off the impending interview. Hopefully the wait will not be too long, but there can be delay and it is worth considering taking along something to read.

Feeling nervous whilst waiting is quite natural: wondering what questions are going to be asked; wondering if the 'right' answers will come easily. There is, however, no need to be apprehensive. Just aim to be yourself and you are likely to make the best impression. Trying to act a part reduces your ability to concentrate. A few deep breaths will ease the tension.

When the Interview Begins

It helps to remember that the interviewer might also be nervous, firstly about appearing efficient and secondly about ensuring that a good choice of new employee is made. The interviewer also has to conduct the proceedings and will take the initiative in shaking hands and offering a seat. Some casual comments usually follow as ice breakers.

You will make a favourable impression if you appear interested and relaxed without being overconfident or laid back. Sitting up and sitting still with your hands in your lap is a good posture to adopt. Fiddling with jewellery or some item of clothing creates a poor impression.

During the Interview

The preliminary casual remarks quickly lead into the interview proper. Interviewers often go through the application form in order to find out more but also to encourage the applicant to talk. A good interviewer will therefore ask open-ended questions which require more than a 'yes' or 'no' answer. Unfortunately some interviewers are not very good at this. You might have to work hard in order to elaborate on the 'yes' or 'no' which appears to be all that is necessary as an answer.

Paying attention to what is being asked, listening carefully, answering fully, and to the point, will obviously gain approval. If you are already in work, be prepared for questions about it: the type of work, your responsibilities, in what way it could be seen as preparation for the post you are applying for, and why you now want to move on.

Ambitions and why the 'new' job appeals are likely topics whether you are already working or just starting work. If the latter, your expectations might be explored in an effort to determine whether or not your ideas of what might be involved are realistic. If the former, it is best not to exaggerate your previous experience but equally not to be diffident about it, or about qualifications or qualities which appear appropriate. Making the most of what you have to offer is what it is all about. Try not to be on the defensive and avoid running a present employer down. This indicates disloyalty and might be thought of as an attitude which could be turned against a new employer.

Be alert to the interviewer's responses. Nodding obviously indicates agreement with what you are saying and a willingness to listen to more. If the interviewer looks at a clock, possibly you are talking too much. An interruption may mean that you have said enough on that topic, or that it is of no consequence.

Most interviewers will be favourably impressed if you appear businesslike, with facts to hand and expectations thought through. You can do this by not waffling or giving vague answers and by trying to relate your past experience to your expectations of the post for which you are applying.

The interviewer has to decide which applicants appear to have an aptitude for the job on offer. This has to be judged from manner as well as from what is said. It is advisable not to interrupt, even when you are keen to answer. If you are too quick to respond you may give an impression of not having thought about the matter sufficiently. Conversely, if you do not know something there is no shame in saying so. You cannot be expected to know everything.

Gathering More Information

The interviewer should give extra information about the job: its place in the firm and the duties and responsibilities it carries. In addition, details about the workplace such as machinery and equipment used, the type of office and the number of people in it are all things you need to know, and things you should ask questions about if the information is not offered. Quite often a guided tour of the workplace is incorporated in the interview arrangements, and this usually covers these points.

As already mentioned, at some stage towards the end of the interview there should be an opportunity to ask questions of the interviewer on any aspect. It is important to use this opportunity not only as an additional means of making a good impression but also to clarify anything unclear. It is only by knowing exactly what to expect that you can make a decision as to whether or not to accept the job, if it is offered to you. Sometimes people feel foolish asking questions about something which has already been discussed, but it is far more foolish not to ask.

It is quite usual for notes to be taken during an interview, but a good interviewer will try to reduce this to a minimum, possibly by using a checklist, in order to focus his or her attention on the applicant.

Competence Builder 3   (Element 8.2)

If you are at college or in training, ask your tutor if it is possible to arrange for mock interviews and/or ask your friends and relatives to tell you about interviews they have had. This will help you to get a 'feel' for them.

The End of the Interview

This is likely to be signified by the interviewer thanking you for attending and stating that a letter regarding the outcome will be sent as soon as possible. This is not a polite way of turning you down, but simply indicates that time is needed in order to make a final decision, or that there are other applicants to be considered. Sometimes an offer of the job is made on the spot, or you might be told that you were not successful. In this case you might be given a reason or offered some advice which could be helpful for future interviews and therefore be worth remembering.

If you are offered a job on the spot, you should not necessarily accept it automatically there and then. During the interview new information about the job will have emerged and it might be wise to consider it. Unless you are absolutely certain that the job is without doubt the right one, it is safest to indicate pleasure and interest and to say that you would appreciate a day or two to think it over. This is quite normal, and if the interviewer is sure enough to offer the job immediately this is not likely to be altered for the sake of a short delay. An immediate acceptance could reasonably be expected, however, if you were sent detailed information in advance of the interview.

If it is agreed that an answer can be deferred, then you must make a decision within the agreed time period, whether it be 'yes' or 'no'. Apart from the fact that it is discourteous to delay, if you decide not to accept the employer will probably want to contact and offer the job to someone previously turned down or still waiting to hear.

AWAITING RESULTS

This is the tough part! It is hard to avoid going over the interview in your mind, agonising over the omission of some vital point or something you now wish you had not said. Remember that you are likely to be exaggerating out of all proportion something that will probably not affect the outcome.

You can turn such a 'post mortem' to advantage. Make a few notes soon after the interview, recording your wrong moves. This will help you to remember and thus avoid them in the future.

Competence Builder 4   *(Element 8.2)*

Make notes after any interview – real or mock – and keep them for reference to help you to improve your performance at some future time.

It is not unreasonable to expect a firm to make a decision quickly, but if there were a number of applicants interviewed, and on different days, it might take some time to get through them all and then make a decision. Firms are also aware that sometimes the first choice applicant turns the job down; they therefore await a decision from this person before notifying the unsuccessful applicants.

You will find the waiting easier if you continue your job seeking. This may even lead to a choice! How do you decide what to do if this happens? What should influence your decision?

If the choice is not obvious, then a way out of the dilemma is to make a list of what you hope to get from a job and of what is important to you. Compare the jobs offered against this. Ask yourself: is it interest, status or good prospects for promotion that matter most? Is pay important (not just what is offered immediately but how quickly and to what extent it will rise in the future)? Would you have to travel to and from work? This can be costly and time-consuming. What do you know about the boss and other people working for the firm?

Eventually the waiting comes to an end with the arrival of the anxiously awaited letter. If it is a rejection you will naturally be disappointed, but remember that to have got an interview is in itself an achievement. A turndown does not in any event indicate that you lack the desired qualities or qualifications. Applying for a job means competing with others, some of whom might have had more relevant experience.

A formal offer of a job will give details such as starting date, hours of work, holiday entitlement, salary, etc. You should reply to this immediately in a formal manner either repeating the terms of employment or stating acceptance of them as laid down in the letter. If you decide to decline the offer, your reply should be equally prompt. There is no need to give a reason unless you wish to do so, but this is usually appreciated.

Competence Builder 5 *(Elements 2.4, 3.1)*

Type two letters, one accepting a job, one turning down the offer of one.

If you accept the job, there just remains the waiting time before the first day. If you are starting a first job, this time can be usefully spent in brushing up your skills to make as good a beginning as possible. First impressions are very important.

LEAVING THE OLD JOB

If you are changing jobs, then you will have to write a letter formally giving notice of your intention to leave your present employer. You will also have to work through the appropriate length of time for notice. It is not the easiest period. There is the excitement and anticipation of the new job, and this can make what you are leaving behind seem unimportant. But, looking ahead, you might need the old employer as a referee at some future job seeking time. For this reason, as well as for the satisfaction of having done a job well, it is worth making an effort to clear up all outstanding work and, where appropriate, ensure a smooth handing over to the next person.

Competence Builder 6 *(Elements 2.4, 3.1)*

For practice, type a letter formally giving notice of your intention to leave your present, or an imagined, post. Discuss the appropriateness of what you have stated with your tutor or a colleague who has previously changed jobs.

UNIT 12

The New Job

The offer of a new job is exhilarating. You see opportunities stretching out ahead and new challenges on the horizon. Unfortunately, these good feelings are often dampened by the realities of the first few days in a new post. They can be disappointing, bewildering, and a time of much heartsearching as to whether or not you have made the right decision. Disappointments can arise from the type of work you are given to do and/or the working relationships you have to establish. You might have to accept that one or the other may not be exactly as you would wish.

FIRST IMPRESSIONS

It is important to be aware that it is not unusual for new jobs to be initially disappointing. It is also important to recognise the reasons why, because success in coping with this period has a direct bearing on how well you settle in and are accepted. What matters is making a good first impression. This is vital, but not easy in an unfamiliar environment and where people have already got their established positions and work routines.

If it is your first job, you will need to make the additional adjustment to a longer working day, which is not necessarily broken up into the short periods of differing activities which you might have been used to. At the beginning you might also find that there is not enough work to do and much of what you have learnt is not being used. You cannot, however, expect to become more satisfyingly employed until you have learnt the daily routine basics. Much of what there is to do in the early days can be very simple, but this is unlikely to be typical of what the job will become. It is usually just a matter of allowing time to become sufficiently familiar with the work in order to take on responsibility for it. Greater involvement, greater interest will then follow.

For some people the new job continues to be a disappointment. This might be because of misunderstanding at interview or of unrealistic expectations. It is very easy to be so carried away with having actually got a job that you forget to think about the realities of working. Some mismatches in expectations are minor, others more serious. It is usually worth waiting to see how the job as a whole turns out before you make an issue of it. What is unexpected and unwelcome at the beginning may turn out to be more interesting in the long run.

ESTABLISHING RELATIONSHIPS

Making a good start is a two-way process. Established staff are likely to appraise critically anyone new, trying to determine whether or not that person will 'fit in' or if any of their established ways are likely to be upset.

As noted in Unit 8, colleagues may come from different backgrounds and have differing ideas and viewpoints. Also, the age range might be wider than you expected and, if you are fresh from college, you might miss the 'matiness' of student days. Usually it is possible to find someone at work with whom you can be friendly, but it is wise to take it steady before becoming too involved. It is not easy to cool or drop an unsatisfactory friendship when it is with a close work colleague.

IN CONCLUSION

In so many ways, what you get out of work is determined by how much you put into it. Most jobs in business administration provide opportunities to learn more than the minimum needed to fulfil requirements, and to observe how people in senior posts go about their work. If you are observant and put into practice what you have learnt, you will be able to prove your competence in some tasks at higher levels and thereby be ready for promotion should an opportunity arise.

Continuing Competence Builder

You have been asked many times in the Competence Builders to undertake tasks which will have shown what you are good at and what you have difficulties with. Think about these. Draw up separate lists of your strengths and weaknesses. Use what you are good at. Try to overcome your weaknesses, don't let them defeat you. Take all the opportunities that come along, or that you can make for yourself. Don't let anything deter or prevent you from climbing as far up the working ladder as you want – or as far as it is possible for you – to go. If you strive to be truly competent this could be a long way.

Appendix

BUSINESS ADMINISTRATION LEVEL 1 STANDARDS – UNIT AND ELEMENT STRUCTURE

UNIT 1   **Filing**

Element 1.1 File documents and open new files within an established filing system (pp. 3–8, 9–12)

1.2 Identify and retrieve documents from within an established filing system (pp. 3–6, 8–9, 9–12)

UNIT 2   **Communicating Information**

Element 2.1 Process incoming and outgoing business telephone calls (pp. 13–20)

2.2 Receive and relay oral and written messages (pp. 20–4)

2.3 Supply information for a specific purpose (pp. 24–8)

2.4 Draft routine business communications (pp. 28–32)

UNIT 3   **Data Processing**

Element 3.1 Produce alpha/numerical information in typewritten form (pp. 33–6)

3.2 Identify and mark errors on scripted material, for correction (pp. 35–7)

3.3 Update records in a computerised database (pp. 38–40)

UNIT 4   **Processing Petty Cash and Invoices**

Element 4.1 Process petty cash transactions (pp. 41–6)

4.2 Process incoming invoices for payment (pp. 46–9)

UNIT 5   **Stock Handling**

Element 5.1 Issue office materials on request and monitor stock levels (pp. 50–7)

UNIT 6   **Mail Handling**

Element 6.1 Receive, sort and distribute incoming/internal mail (pp. 58–60, 61–2)

6.2 Prepare for despatch outgoing/internal mail (pp. 60–2)

UNIT 7   **Reprographics**

Element 7.1 Produce copies from original documents using reprographic equipment (pp. 63–6)

UNIT 8   **Liaising with Callers and Colleagues**

Element 8.1 Receive and assist callers (pp. 67–70, 72–3)

       8.2 Maintain business relationships with other members of staff (pp. 70–3)

UNIT 9   **Health and Safety**

Element 9.1 Operate safely in the workplace (pp. 74–80 and throughout the text)